Shakespeare in Performance

Shakespeare in Performance
A Collection of Essays

Edited by
Frank Occhiogrosso

Newark: University of Delaware Press
London: Associated University Presses

© 2003 by Rosemont Publishing & Printing Corp.

All rights reserved. Authorization to photocopy items for internal or personal use, or the internal or personal use of specific clients, is granted by the copyright owner, provided that a base fee of $10.00, plus eight cents per page, per copy is paid directly to the Copyright Clearance Center, 222 Rosewood Drive, Danvers, Massachusetts 01923. [0-87413-776-4/03 $10.00 + 8 ¢ pp, pc.]

Other than as indicated in the foregoing, this book may not be reproduced, in whole or in part, in any form (except as permitted by Sections 107 and 108 of the U.S. Copyright Law, and except for brief quotes appearing in reviews in the public press.)

Associated University Presses
2010 Eastpark Boulevard
Cranbury, NJ 08512

Associated University Presses
16 Barter Street
London WC1A 2AH, England

Associated University Presses
P.O. Box 338, Port Credit
Mississauga, Ontario
Canada L5G 4L8

The paper used in this publication meets the requirements of the American National Standard for Permanence of Paper for Printed Library Materials Z39.48-1984.

Library of Congress Cataloging-in-Publication Data

Shakespeare in performance : a collection of essays / edited by Frank Occhiogrosso.
   p. cm.
  Includes bibliographical references and index.
  ISBN 0-87413-776-4
  1. Shakespeare, William, 1564–1616—Dramatic production. 2. Shakespeare, William, 1564–1616—Stage history—1950– I. Occhiogrosso, Frank, 1943–

PR3091 .S3627 2003
792.9'5—dc21

2002018093

Contents

Introduction Frank Occhiogrosso	7
Shakespeare in Performance, Study, and Criticism John Russell Brown	15
Shylock, Antonio, and the Politics of Performance James C. Bulman	27
The Merchant of Venice Ralph Berry	47
Romeo and Juliet in Performance Jay L. Halio	58
"I have done the deed": *Macbeth* 2.2 James P. Lusardi and June Schlueter	71
Disguise in Trevor Nunn's *Twelfth Night* H. R. Coursen	84
Storm, Fire, and Blood: Patterns of Imagery in Stuart Burge's *Julius Caesar* Harry Keyishian	93
Teaching What's Not There Alan C. Dessen	104
The New Globe Pauline Kiernan	113
Tracking Performance Criticism of Shakespeare Marvin Rosenberg	123
Bibliography	137
List of Contributors	141
Index	143

Introduction

Frank Occhiogrosso

WITH ONE EXCEPTION, ALL OF THE ESSAYS IN THIS VOLUME WERE PRESENTED, some of them in slightly altered form, at a conference entitled "Shakespeare in Performance" at Drew University in June of 1999. The presenters at that conference, each of them a recognized authority on some aspect of Shakespearean performance criticism or scholarship, were asked to read (and illustrate) a paper that dealt with performance as a mode of critical approach to and interpretation of Shakespeare. Furthermore, each presenter was asked to direct his/her remarks, where applicable, to teachers of Shakespeare and to the use of performance as a pedagogical tool. All but one of the essays that follow are the results of this endeavor, the one exception being Marvin Rosenberg's essay "Tracking Performance Criticism of Shakespeare," which has been written specially for this book.

Shakespearean performance studies contain several differing though connected areas of concern. The first is stage history, represented by such books as G. C. D. Odell's *Shakespeare From Betterton to Irving*, J. C. Trewin's *Shakespeare on the English Stage, 1900–1964*, Robert Speaight's *Shakespeare on the Stage*, and more recently, Jonathan Bate and Russell Jackson's *Shakespeare, An Illustrated Stage History*. A second area is physical playhouse scholarship, which includes books on the Globe and Blackfriars by J. C. Adams, C. W. Hodges, Irwin Smith, Richard Hosley, John Orrell, and perhaps most apt, recent publications on the new Globe such as J. R. Mulryne and Margaret Shewring's *Shakespeare's Globe Rebuilt*. A third area deals with the staging of plays in the Elizabethan theater such as can be found in the books of Bernard Beckerman, Andrew Gurr, and Alan Dessen. And finally there is what is perhaps the richest area of exploration, that which studies performance itself and therefore pays close attention to what actors, directors, and designers do and have done to the Shakespearean playtext in translating it to stage or screen. This sizeable field begins with Harley Granville-Barker and A. C. Sprague, and moves up through the studies of Marvin Rosenberg and John Russell Brown, to discussions by the actors and directors themselves, such as those contained in volumes by John Barton and Carol Rutter, and in the Cambridge *Players of Shakespeare* series. This field is given theoretical discussion in such recent books as *Shakespeare, Theory, and Performance*, edited by James Bulman, and William Worthen's *Shakespeare and the Authority of Performance*.

The first essay in this volume, as it was also the opening address at the conference, is John Russell Brown's "Shakespeare in Performance, Study, and Criticism." It is an essay which challenges us to encounter Shakespeare not as stable text but as unstable performance, an essay that Brown, by virtue of his several books on Shakespeare in performance as well as his having lived a life in the theater, is eminently qualified to write. Anticipating Marvin Rosenberg's essay (which ends this volume) on the nature of Shakespearean performance studies, Brown writes of the efforts of directors, actors, theater historians, physical playhouse scholars, and critics to come at Shakespeare from a theatrical rather than a purely literary perspective. He provides an ably informed summary of the kinds of issues that have been central to performance studies, as well as the various modes of approach employed. As such his essay constitutes not only an apt opening for this collection, but also an equally apt point of departure for the next stage of Shakespearean performance studies, because he challenges the reader to consider the *standards* by which performance can be evaluated, standards which have not yet been defined or established.

The next six essays are on specific plays: James Bulman on *The Merchant of Venice*, Ralph Berry, also on *Merchant*, Jay Halio on *Romeo and Juliet*, James Lusardi and June Schlueter on *Macbeth*, Herbert Coursen on *Twelfth Night*, and Harry Keyishian on *Julius Caesar*.

James Bulman, editor of the *Shakespeare's Plays in Performance* series and, more recently, editor of a volume on theory as applied to performance, gives here a stage history of *The Merchant of Venice*. It is especially valuable not only because of its inclusion (in fact, its heavily emphasizing) of productions from the 1990s, but also because of its consideration of the implications of the shift in emphasis, in many recent productions, from Shylock to Antonio. Bulman's is a stage history that will be very useful to teachers of the play wishing to contextualize discussions of Shylock and Antonio, as well as to performance critics and scholars generally.

Ralph Berry, in his essay on *The Merchant*, takes up the question of setting, i.e., Renaissance or modern, and makes a good case for setting the play in Renaissance Venice based upon an examination of several recent productions of the play. From a Fascist 1930s Italy setting complete with black-shirted thugs, to a 1980s London setting emphasizing banking and the stock exchange, Berry comes to several productions that emphasize the physical aspects of Renaissance Venice, especially its Jewish ghetto, arguing that a setting that displays "the uneasy collaboration of Christians and Jews" is most apt for the play's deep ambiguities.

Jay Halio, expert in the business of editing Shakespeare's text, brings that specialized expertise to bear upon performance in *Romeo and Juliet*. Beginning with Q1, the much-maligned and so-called "bad" quarto, Halio traces the history of the play in performance from the eighteenth century to the present, noting along the way Garrick's alterations of the play, as well as Kemble's, Cushman's and others', all of whom made cuts that seem to follow those in Q1. In addition to the cutting of the playscript, Halio also addresses once again such questions as setting (modern dress vs. period) and directorial concept. He ultimately brings his argument into line with William Worthen's idea of performance "authority" or authenticity, and, like Worthen, holds that authority lies not in fidelity to every word of the original playscript but rather in a "modern idiom" for the play found by every age's directors that brings the play, through performance, to the timeless.

James Lusardi and June Schlueter, the editors of *Shakespeare Bulletin*, the journal of Shakespearean performance criticism, here combine on a discussion of *Macbeth* that is specially geared to pedagogical effectiveness through performance. They focus on 2.2, the murder scene, and in doing so examine the multiple possibilities for acting Macbeth and Lady Macbeth as they react to the king's murder. Schlueter and Lusardi are underscoring what so many of the other performance critics in this volume also note, i.e., the richness of the Shakespearean playtext in opportunities for the actor because of the ambiguity of so many moments in that playtext. Each of these multiple possibilities for interpretation by the actors forces us, the readers/spectators, to see things afresh.

The next three essays deal with film versions of Shakespearean plays and consider the special qualities of cinematic performance, especially the possibilities for teaching the plays. Herbert Coursen, whose many publications include examination of Shakespeare on film and television, looks closely at the Trevor Nunn *Twelfth Night* and the motif of disguise as employed in it by Viola. In the prose of a poet, Coursen lyrically analyzes Nunn's movie, and in the process rings all the changes possible on the motif of gender as represented by Viola's disguising as Cesario. A teacher using Coursen's essay as a guide to teaching *Twelfth Night* by means of Nunn's film has a richly nuanced and sophisticated journey ahead of him/her. Harry Keyishian, who has also written elsewhere on filmed productions of Shakespeare, here focuses on the largely ignored Stuart Burge film of *Julius Caesar* and examines the translation into cinematic terms of the verbal images of storm, fire, and blood in the play. Keyishian looks at mise-en-scene, composition, and montage as features of filmic performance, all of which make for interpretation of the play. Finally, Alan Dessen, a theater historian and playhouse and performance scholar, here turns his attention to several different Shakespearean films in order to highlight the cuts made in the playtext by cinematic directors and the pedagogical use that can be made of considering the effects of and reasons for such omissions, the possibilities inherent in "teaching what's not there."

Mention of playhouse scholarship brings to mind the single most interesting experiment of that kind in our time, namely the new Globe in London, hence the presence in this collection of Pauline Kiernan's essay on the new Globe. A scholar-in-residence on bankside, Kiernan has been in an excellent position to comment on how, for the performance critic and scholar, the discoveries made in acting Shakespeare at the new Globe fit into the overall scheme of performance studies concerns. Her interviews with the actors and directors add a special dimension to the actors' viewpoint branch of performance studies, because here the actors' viewpoint is modified by the unique physical conditions of performance at the new Globe.

Finally, the volume concludes with Marvin Rosenberg's "Tracking Performance Criticism of Shakespeare," written specially for this collection. Rosenberg, who has developed over the years and through five important books his own approach to Shakespeare performance study, here gives us a prolegomenon to a history of Shakespearean performance criticism. He does so by establishing the principle of *variousness* of the art of the actor (as opposed to uniformity, as Harbage and Joseph had thought), the centrality of the actor's natural discovery of the basis in feeling for what in the playtext he is acting. Drawing on his own experience in the theater, Rosenberg points out that the actor's art is physical, imaginative, and personal, and therefore well suited to the *polyphony*—to use Rosenberg's own celebrated term—found in all the great Shakespearean characters. Rosenberg discusses the emergence of stage history as a fundamental branch of performance study, and he emphasizes the key role, in this emerging mode, of A. C. Sprague's study of stage business in Shakespeare, bringing the nonscripted element into critical discussion, where it has remained as a central concern of Shakespearean performance criticism. But it is to the polyphony in Shakespeare's characters, matched by the varied art of the actor, to which Rosenberg consistently returns, and in doing so he underscores perhaps better than anyone how what Bulman and Worthen call the instability of the Shakespearean text is well served by Shakespearean performance criticism.

This collection of essays is rich and varied. It touches upon all of the areas of Shakespearean performance studies mentioned above. And it presents essays by some of the foremost scholars and critics working in this important field today. Finally, every one of these essays will be of use to the teacher who wishes to use performance as a mode of entry into the text of Shakespeare, wherein all the world's a stage.

Shakespeare in Performance

Shakespeare in Performance, Study, and Criticism

John Russell Brown

Shakespeare took great pleasure in the use of words and wrestled with them so that he could define his thoughts for others to understand and communicate his feelings that would otherwise be intensely private and soon lost forever. For all these reasons, Shakespeare's plays have been studied as literature: they have become mines full of amazing arguments, examples of writing to be pondered, specimens to be carefully dissected and analyzed. Professors of English write about the texts; students of English language and literature study them; poets echo them. No library is without a copy of all thirty-six or -seven of them. New editions come out year after year and publishers profit endlessly. Shakespeare's words are popular, too; quotations are everywhere, on newsstands and billboards, in political speeches and sermons, and in our lovemaking; a phrase or two taken from Shakespeare may meet us at any time in almost any circumstance.

But all this does a disservice to Shakespeare's texts, because it misuses them. They were not written to be read, either silently or aloud; they were meant to be part of entire plays acted by actors on a stage before audiences. Words on a page do not represent what Shakespeare thought and felt, how he responded to his life and times, what he imagined life might be, the pleasures he wished to discover and share, the warnings he felt impelled to give; they are only clues to that. Each word should be considered in its full context, with regard to narrative, structure, argument, dramatic situation and character, but that is not all: they should also be considered as part of a reflection of lived experience. Physical presence, movement in space, nervous tension are all part of the illusory world they were written to set in motion. Shakespeare thought of words as they would be embodied by actors, producers, managers, technicians, dressmakers, carpenters, all contributing according to their own skills and their individual identities, life-histories, and social and family backgrounds. For Shakespeare, theater was an arena in which everything that is alive had its role to play so that the effect of any written text on an audience would be changing all the time as it is realized in action, by others as well as by its author. Shakespeare's creativity was such that it could not be represented by words on a page but called for, used, and manipulated a complex image of life that moved and breathed, and drew to itself the responses of all manner of highly skilled and instinctive persons, encouraging them to operate at the height of their powers. He was not only creative in himself, but the cause that creativity is in others.

How can a critic in a library begin to understand how Shakespeare's plays come to life in the theater? How can a student in a classroom, or left to his or her own devices, gain access to the lively image of life that can arise from the words on a page? These are huge questions and in the present century many astute and learned scholars have tried to figure out the answers.

* * *

When we try to understand Shakespeare's texts as a part of plays in performance, we find ourselves faced with the ephemeral as well as the permanent, the sensational along with the well-argued and finely expressed, the tangible with the intellectual. Sight is involved as well as sound, stillness, and movement, effects at a distance and those that are close-up and unavoidable. We must be ready for an adventure into the unknown, where what is familiar will be seen afresh and we may well lose our bearings. This is not a territory for bookworms and, since little is indisputable, not for dogmatists either.

So difficult is the terrain that many have argued it is not worth entering. Words are stable on a page—more or less—so let us stick to that evidence of Shakespeare's greatness and be students of English literature, pure and simple. The vagaries of theater in which the texts are dressed for performance will obscure our view of them, so let us strip away all that accidental accretion. Vulgar entertainment competes with clarity of meaning, so let us cut that part of Shakespeare's concern out of the reckoning when we try to assess his vision of the world. We have quite enough to do when looking closely at his "poetry" or the intellectual subtlety of his arguments, so why look for more? These arguments are attractive to many people, as we can see by rows of books in libraries and scholarly journals thick with footnoted contributions. The texts alone can yield evidence about genres, themes, characters, ideas, ideologies, and, in a bookish sense, images. Words alone can be quoted in debate about content and style without worrying about a theatrical context. Students can be examined and their teachers' careers promoted by means of responsible and innovative research that is solely literary in its techniques. Why sully enjoyment or cloud understanding by reference to performance with all its uncertain and catch-penny ways? Our critical arguments can be home and dry without having to encounter any such difficulties as stages, actors, time, space, audiences, sensations, and emotions.

But to ignore Shakespeare's chosen medium and the use to which he put all his words is a cowardly reaction. It shrinks away from what is palpable and immediately accessible. It does not touch those parts of the plays that have appealed widely and instinctively to millions of men and women in the centuries since they were written. Over the last decades we have come to realize that these plays—not their words alone—can draw audiences with little or no knowledge of the English language or of European thought and culture; the subtlety, imagery, lyricism, humor, intellectual refinement of Shakespeare's words, amazing though these certainly are, cannot account for the global acceptance of what Shakespeare has left us. He wrote plays in which everything that is alive can have a part to play, texts that can be performed in many ways according to the talents and interests of those who perform them, entertainments that appeal to many very different people at many different times. Those who wish to understand the words that Shakespeare wrote as he intended them to be received should try to explain how all this should be.

* * *

In the present century, many persons have tackled the problems of understanding how Shakespeare's plays work in performance and this collection testifies to their success. Back in the 1920s and 1930s, Harley Granville Barker used his experience as actor, director and dramatist to unlock many secrets of the theatrical life of the texts. In the 1940s, Arthur Colby Sprague collected descriptions of the stage-business with which eminent actors had enhanced their performances and interpreted the texts. In the 1960s, Bernard Beckerman marshaled evidence to show how stage action was handled in early performances and its effect on an audience's experience of the plays; Marvin Rosenberg accumulated details of how individual actors had responded to the texts and so demonstrated the many colors and intentions that Shakespeare's words have been given in performance. Throughout the century, some critics working in the mainstream, literary tradition have, occasionally, stretched their sights and offered arguments that refer incidentally to what they have seen on a stage or what they imagine to be the effect of performance: A. C. Bradley, back in 1904, Una Ellis-Fermor, Muriel Bradbrook, Kenneth Muir, and, in the present time, many, many more. Sometimes, we may suspect, an uncritical reference to how a play has been performed by a particular actor or staged by a particular director and designer is used as a blind to stave off the larger questions that arise from the study of a text's theatrical life.

In the last few decades of the twentieth century, however, a huge concourse of scholars and critics have been seriously concerned with what is usually known as "the study of Shakespeare's plays in performance." This has become a great tree with many branches, an industry with a large workforce and many products, a way of enlivening classrooms and inviting students to look and listen as well as read, to encounter and experience as well as receive information and repeat it. In many lines of research and pedagogy, work is in hand and still more is waiting to be done.

Search for the original conditions of performance has led Alan Dessen to ever-closer scrutiny of both texts and early editions, Peter Thomson and Andrew Gurr to a practical concern with the actors' business management. Walter Hodges and, again, Andrew Gurr, with many others, have tried to make precise calculations about the size, structure, materials, and workmanship of Elizabethan playhouses. All this research has achieved an unmissable monument in the new Globe, now up and running on Bankside in London. The methods of rehearsal and production in Shakespeare's day have been the subject of books by Thomas King, Michael Hattaway, Peter Thomson, Keith Sturgess, and David Bradby. Now, the new Globe and other practical explorations are encouraging further studies. Slowly, a better or, at least, a fuller sense is being developed of how the stage practices of Shakespeare's day differed from those current today and, in consequence, the inherent theatrical qualities of the texts are being reassessed.

John Ripley, Dennis Bartholomeusz, Gary Jay Williams and others have studied the stage histories of individual plays. These have been joined by the authors of several series of books, called "Shakespeare in Performance," "Plays in Performance," and "Shakespeare in Production." By disentangling the consequences of various stagings these scholars have built up a synoptic and historical view of each play in performance. Their research has given a big impetus toward comparative study in which one mode of performance or one set of directorial decisions can be measured against others from different times and places. Perhaps the most notable result has been to establish the instability of any effect that Shakespeare's words can be given in the theater: there seems to be no possibility of a definitive production or, even, of getting any one detail "right." However imaginative or skilled any one actor's performance may be, it will not be long before it is superseded with yet more revelations. Stage histories are often books that are bursting at their seams, so much has been found that the writer wants to share and not lose forever in bundles of press clippings, yellowing notes, and computerized data-banks. Our view of what these texts may become in performance is being both deepened and widened; and, in consequence, it has been made insecure.

In the crucial task of studying what the texts require from actors, scholars have been joined by practitioners and theoreticians so that we now know far more about how words become speech and a part of complete performances. Bertram Joseph was early in this field, and notable developments followed from, among others, Michael Goldman, John Barton, Robert Cohen, and William Worthen. Recently, the study of acting in Shakespeare's day has received new impetus from scholars who, for largely untheatrical reasons, have directed a penetrating attention to the questions of how "boy actors" managed to perform the most demanding of female roles and the effect this might have on our understanding of the texts. Scholars and readers who have never been actors, and never want to be, are slowly learning to understand the problems that are faced in rehearsals and performances, and to some extent sharing in them. The "Players of Shakespeare" series has collected personal accounts of how particular roles have been tackled. The actors writing in these books are all of the present day and seldom concerned with how Shakespeare's theater might have presented the plays, but what they say has a practical basis and, often, a blow-by-blow narrative of rehearsals that reveals more than the impressionistic and opinionated descriptions found in the newspaper reviews and interviews which, not long ago, were the primary resource for critics and scholars. A new self-awareness and openness among actors and directors have encouraged them to make considered statements that are eminently quotable by scholars wishing to consider what is usually hidden in rehearsals and behind the scenes. In many ways, the processes of performance are becoming more widely accessible: actors visit campuses and, when we are lucky, conferences take place alongside festival performances.

Because the only performances observable for study are those on the stage at the present time, may scholars are avid theatergoers and some assess their experiences by writing theater reviews. Richard David, Stanley Wells, and Peter Holland have published collections of them that, taken together, cover almost the whole range of British productions since World War II and so are able to develop arguments about the theatrical qualities of the texts and the efficacy of various approaches to acting and directing them. I do not know of comparable books about North American Shakespeare and I suspect that this is because there are too many productions to write about and no clear leader among the companies. Most books about Shakespeare production are general or introductory in scope or limited to particular artists or aspects of production. Dennis Kennedy's *Looking at Shakespeare* (1993) concentrates mostly on the visual aspects of performance, but its range covers the entire twentieth century and the whole of Europe and North America: here is an exceptional book that is a thoroughly comparative study of Shakespeare in the modern theater. It has been followed by studies of Shakespeare production in Germany, Japan, and, soon to be published, in French-speaking Canada, Eastern Europe, India, and China. In step with this work, a comprehensive series, called "Directors in Perspective," has enabled scholars to study, in greater detail than before, the evolution of distinct styles of presentation and rehearsal and to avoid the parochialism and lack of critical distance that experience of only a few theaters can encourage. Evidence from Peter Brook, Giorgio Strehler, Ingmar Bergman, Peter Stein, Robert Lepage and other shrewd and imaginative directors has now been added to the study of Shakespeare's plays in performance. Intimate knowledge of the processes of production in our own time can, with care, be used to discover more about the performative qualities of the texts written for a very different theater with no director in charge to choose and control effects, and with little scope for scenographic marvels to modify and enhance an audience's responses.

* * *

Yet all this effort has proved insufficient to ensure that every scholar and critic of Shakespeare studies the plays in performance. Persuading a literary scholar/critic to consider performance is like trying to convince someone who has never been near any water that it is possible and enjoyable to float and, even, to swim. Perhaps the most serious problem in convincing others to study Shakespeare in the theater has been a lack of widely recognized standards of judgment. How can we know whether what one actor or director chooses to do is faithful, revealing, or damaging to the text, or whether it is just lazy or ignorant? What marks a serious experiment apart from a publicity-conscious stunt? How can we identify the bluff that seeks to hide an absence of skill or imagination? Which of many productions are worthy of attention, and what aspects of those examples? To what research should priority be given at a time when books and articles are emerging in great numbers? Given sufficient space, it is comparatively easy to describe what happens on a stage, but that is not enough. Those who study Shakespeare's plays in performance need to develop clearer standards of judgment if their work is to win widespread acceptance. Of course, there will always be differences of opinion, but generally accepted standards of judgment should be possible for describing how words have been spoken or whether performances and staging are sensitive to the most significant qualities of a text.

Yet even description remains problematic. Present-day literary scholars and critics can often provide very clear statements of their findings: the influence of this social phenomenon, political idea, or theological nicety, on this text or that. They can be logical in argument and clinch their conclusions with neat verbal quotations. Scholars who study Shakespeare's plays in performance can do none of these things and yet they must try to get attention from those to whom they are second nature. I know of no one who can speak of Shakespeare's plays in performance with a conviction to match that of many a literary critic. It cannot be said *how* Hamlet dies, or Lear or Cleopatra, or Juliet and Romeo. We can quote what is said but cannot adequately describe how the words are said in any one performance, nor what effect they have on an audience. Moreover, we cannot know for sure what happens within the speakers, in body as well as mind, and how that effects the force and implications of what is said or what elements of that inward drama communicates to an audience.

For example, how out of breath is King Lear when he is dying and how strongly does he have to struggle in order to speak? This is bound to affect an audience's reaction, as it does in life when we watch an old man during his last moments. When exactly does King Lear stop breathing? Is he looking at Cordelia as he dies or at those who stand around him? Does he believe Cordelia will never breathe again or does he, in imagination, believe that she is alive and will live? How slowly or quickly does anyone respond? How are we encouraged to view the spectacle of his death: can we see him easily or is he obscured by those who are in attendance? Does he know what he is saying or why he is saying it? All these practical matters influence what the tragedy achieves, and they will go on doing so in the audience's imaginations when the stage is empty and there is time to wonder at what has happened and what it all meant. Many questions must be raised in the study of this single moment before we can come to a responsible judgement about what the words that are spoken have achieved.

These problems of performance criticism extend to entire plays. No one can tell me how Benedick and Beatrice should first meet, what they think and what they do, how close they are to each other, and so on, but still less can we be sure of the effect of following them through the whole play as they talk and quarrel, fall silent or laugh, or cry out in speechless anguish or joy. About their verbal jests and misunderstandings we can be sure of our ground, but not about *why* these people in the play are witty. Nor do we know why any one quibble or image comes to mind when it does. Perhaps we can be sure what Beatrice means when she says that, were she a man, she would eat Claudio's heart in the market place—although I am far from sure to what extent she actually envisions doing so—but that information does not explain why, at this stage in the play, she pays no attention to what Benedick is trying to say or, at least, gives no spoken sign that she hears him. Nor does it tell us whether, at this moment, she tries to behave like a man, or her idea of a man. Does Beatrice know how extreme she is being when she talks of eating a man's heart? What are the motives that make her want to be a man? Why does she move from questions to explanations, and on to assertions? What does the audience *see* as it hears the words? What physical emphasis is given to the expression of Beatrice's fury: how confident is her bearing, do her eyes shine, is her voice hard, penetrating, or loud? All these issues and more are involved with acting Shakespeare's text at this moment so that it arises as a necessary development of the role far into the play. How an actor resolves them will affect an audience, perhaps more deeply (because more instinctively) than the words alone could ever do in all their complexities and simplicities. Acting is what brings the text alive to an audience in terms that it recognizes from its own lived experiences: it speaks in a language that is physical and sensuous, as well as verbal; and it is thoroughly involved with motivation and emotion.

To consider the effect of this comedy in performance, standards of judgement are urgently needed. How can we know which way of acting is most suitable to the text, most responsive, not only to the words that are being spoken at any one moment, but also to all the others throughout the entire role of Beatrice, her relationship to other characters, and the development of the comic action. How can any study discriminate between the myriad possibilities of enactment? These are problems for the study of Shakespeare's plays in performance that are, I believe, unanswerable at the present time. Perhaps we should seek out those performances that seem to speak most directly to ourselves in the world in which we find ourselves and answer only from our own responses to those. We would all give different answers, but at least we would be studying the plays as they relate to the one world of which we have first-hand experience. That, however, might well leave us speaking only to ourselves and we would be at the mercy of those performances to which we happen to have access.

Another recourse would be to concentrate on trying to recover the kinds of staging and performance for which Shakespeare was writing. That is a long and uncertain road, since it is difficult to imagine performances that we have never seen and audience reactions which we can never share. Moreover, one of the certainties about Shakespeare's plays is that the style in which they are written changes from play to play, so presumably we would be seeking to identify several different kinds of performance.

* * *

Questions of validity and judgement are being actively pursued at the present time in at least three distinct ways. First of all, a new subject, called performance studies, has been established in numerous universities which is concerned with what happens in any performance, within the performer and among his or her audience. We are learning how to describe the physical and psychological elements of acting, the use of space and time, the reflections and distortions of reality, the influence of production procedures and place of performance. With theater history to help, we are beginning to distinguish between varieties of rehearsal and performance, observe changing relationships between performer and performance, and between performer and audience, and to ask what part a performer's individual history and personal characteristics of mind and body have upon any role that he or she undertakes. We have learned to recognize the influence of earlier performances by individual actors and of different modes of preparation and rehearsal. In performance studies our knowledge of acting has entered a new phase and may, perhaps, help us to a better understanding of the demands made by Shakespeare's exceptional texts and their opportunities for variable enactment.

Secondly, in schools of cultural studies and in departments of sociology and psychology, audiences and audience-reactions are being studied with an urgency that has been fueled by the interest arising from rapid growth of electronic media. Theories of perception, sensation, and phenomenology are being developed and can be used to describe what happens when a play is performed. Data is being collected about social and cultural conditioning of audiences, fueled by a political and moral interest in a multiracial society and in intracultural achievements. Not all this research and theorizing is entirely new—theater historians and Shakespeare scholars have long been interested in the composition of audiences and their responses to particular plays—but a wealth of new facts and a vocabulary that is almost entirely new can now be brought to bear on problems intimately connected with the performance of Shakespeare's texts.

Thirdly, yet another new topic of research is gaining a foothold in universities, especially in Scandinavia, Israel, and the Netherlands. "The theatrical event" is being studied as a unique phenomenon with the result that the context in which to describe Shakespeare's plays in performance has been both enlarged and more thoroughly documented and analyzed. The event of a performance involves more than a familiar text and its staging, acting, audience and theater building. It is also greatly influenced by the administrative and cultural context in which the play is presented and by what has happened immediately before the performance to both actors and audience, in their personal lives and shared activities, in their individual education, training, in social conditioning, in political, personal and idealistic aspirations, and so on. To study a performance of a play as part of a theatrical event is to study the interaction of many persons, as members of various groups and as individuals at a particular time and place. While a play may or may not reflect the lives of an audience, its performance will always be a part of their lived experience and so speak in ways that draw upon a large, and largely unconscious, field of thought and sensation. Study of a theatrical event does not have the same close focus as performance studies or audience research, but it does define a field of reference that any criticism of Shakespeare's plays in performance would be more persuasive for taking into account. Perhaps its most important feature is a concern with particular performances rather than a production that runs for weeks or months at a time: each time a play is performed it will be different, because actors and audiences will always have changed since the previous occasion, and each of these events will have something distinct to reveal about the inherent qualities of the text. In studying Shakespeare's plays in performance, it could be more profitable to see one production a number of times than to seek out many different productions, because in this way we might learn more about a text's potential for change, regardless of any one set of choices by actors and director.

* * *

I had no intention of making the study of Shakespeare's plays in performance sound formidably difficult and interminable, but I must point out that this is what it can become. After all, works of art that have such long-lasting and general validity are not likely to yield their secrets easily, still less when the material of which they are made is so infinitely variable and so dependent on many collaborators before reaching the public. To be sure of what we say and what we judge to be right and inevitable about Shakespeare's plays in performance, we would have to be very careful and utilize many ways of study, but the other side of this coin is equally important: whatever moves us or sets our minds racing, or gives us unexpected or acute pleasure during the performance of a Shakespeare play, should be studied with careful attention as part of the far greater whole that can only slowly come into view. The most far-fetched research and subtlest criticism must always return to the momentary hold that these plays can have over the imagination of audiences. We are all privileged witnesses to the life of the plays and our personal and, perhaps, unusual perceptions are necessary parts of any understanding of what Shakespeare achieved. He was not only creative in himself, but the cause that creativity was in others and, in this happy conjunction, critics and students, like audiences and actors, can begin to respond to the great wealth that is on offer.

Shylock, Antonio, and the Politics of Performance

James C. Bulman

THE STUDY OF SHAKESPEARE IN PERFORMANCE STANDS IN A RATHER contentious relationship to poststructuralist theory. To a degree, the dramatic text may be treated as any other literary text, authored not only by Shakespeare but by cultural forces that silently inscribed themselves at the time of its writing. Its meaning, furthermore, is said to be never intrinsic, but always unstable, subject to historical circumstances and to the ideological bias of the reader—feminist, cultural materialist, new historicist, deconstructionist. A dramatic text, therefore, acquires meaning depending on the questions one asks of it. But performance adds another layer, for an audience at a play interacts not just with a dramatic text, as a reader might with a novel, but with interpreters of that text—middlemen: directors, actors, designers—who intervene in an audience's experience of the play and create what Marco De Marinis calls the "performance text," which can be decoded in much the same way words on a page can be.[1] The performance text changes each time a play is staged, and so the significance of a play will change too, according to the contingencies of performance—the intersection of social and political contexts, material conditions, theatrical variables, and audience composition, which will destabilize any fixed value one may be tempted to assign to that text. Making meaning in a theater is thus a collaborative and historically particular enterprise. Performance criticism attempts to recuperate how meaning has been made—how stagings of a play have achieved cultural significance at particular moments in history—in order to discover why Shakespeare has continued to speak with authority over time and across national borders.

In the following pages, I shall illustrate the process by which performances of Shakespeare acquire cultural capital by looking at the stage history of *The Merchant of Venice*, and particularly at the fortunes of Shylock and Antonio. There is reason to believe that in 1596 or 1597, when *Merchant* was first performed, Shylock was played as caricatured Jew.

The description of Shylock's appearance in a ballad written by an actor in the 1630s suggests that he was modeled on the figure of Judas in Corpus Christi plays:

> His beard was red; his face was made
>   Not much unlike a witches.
> His habit was a Jewish gown
>   That would defend all weather;
> His chin turn'd up, his nose hung down,
>   And both ends met together.[2]

Even if one discredits this poem as an unreliable source, there is ample evidence in the text to suggest Shylock's villainy: his miserliness, his lust for a pound of Christian flesh, his running up and down the Rialto bemoaning the loss of his ducats and his daughter, his whetting a knife on his shoe at the trial. Shylock reveals his motives in an early aside to the audience, when he spies Antonio:

> I hate him for he is a Christian;
> But more, for that in low simplicity
> He lends out money gratis, and brings down
> The rate of usance here with us in Venice.
> If I can catch him once upon the hip,
> I will feed fat the ancient grudge I bear him.
>   (1.3.34–39)[3]

By the 1590s, of course, Jews who openly practiced their faith had not lived in England for over three hundred years, having been expelled by Edward I in 1290; and although a few hundred real or pretended converts to Christianity remained, anti-Semitic myths had been able to grow and prosper largely unimpeded by the presence of Jews to refute them. Most widespread was the myth of child murder: Jews were said to steal Christian children, crucify them, and use the blood in the Passover ritual. One hundred and fifty such cases were reported, the most notorious being the death of young Hugh of Lincoln, recounted in the tale told by Chaucer's Prioress. Another popular myth was that Jews caused the black death by poisoning wells and such like. The fact that some converted Jews were doctors perpetuated the myth, and it contributed even as late as 1594 to the frenzy surrounding the case of Roderigo Lopez, a Portugese Jew who, as physician to the queen, was put to death for attempting to poison her.[4]

In the view of many Elizabethans, usury and Judaism were virtually synonymous. The advent of a money economy, the decay of the old aristocratic houses, chronic borrowing, and thrift sapped by the availability of easy credit all produced tensions within Elizabethan society. The moneylender, according to Wilbur Sanders, "though merely the economic instrument of new desires, had all the resultant tensions and crises laid to his door; and the money-lender was, by an ineradicable popular association, the Jew."[5] Historical circumstances explain the association. Jews had been allowed to lend money at interest because Christians were forbidden to do so: the gospels taught that it was wrong to lend for gain, and people still assented to Aristotle's belief that it was unnatural for money to breed more money. This belief underlies Antonio's attack on Shylock for taking "a breed for barren metal" (1.3.126). "[I]s your gold and silver ewes and rams?" he asks, implicitly pointing out the disparity between natural and unnatural increase, to which Shylock wryly replies, "I cannot tell, I make it breed as fast" (87–88).

Like Antonio, Elizabethans commonly condemned usurers as wolves, devils, and heretics: they were "greedie cormoraunte wolves in deede, that rauyn vp both beaste and man" according to *A Discourse upon Usury* (1572); their "houses were called the devils houses, his fields the devils croppe," according to *The Death of Usury, or, The Disgrace of Usurers* (1594). Gratiano uses similar terms at the trial to discredit Shylock: "O be thou damned, inexecrable dog" (4.1.128); "Thy currish spirit / Governed a wolf" (133–34); "thy desires / Are wolfish, bloody, starved, and ravenous" (137–38). Behind such virulence lay the fear that capitalism itself might be ungodly. Were the old religion and the new mercantilism fully compatible? Was the "thrifty" pursuit of trade distinguishable from the "prodigal" indulgence of greed?[6] As an emergent economic power, England of course placed a great value on her merchants, and usury was necessary to ensure that their ventures could thrive. Furthermore, not only merchants, but parliament and the queen herself sought the resources of usurers—virtually none of whom in fact was a Jew;[7] and the queen, by placing a ceiling of 10 percent on lending rates, officially condoned the practice. Usury and trade thus existed in an embarrassing symbiotic relationship, and Shylock became a convenient scapegoat for Shakespeare's Christian audience, bearing the burden of their guilt and mythologizing an evil—greed—from which they wished to dissociate themselves.[8]

***

During the course of the next two centuries, actors who portrayed Shylock seldom elicited sympathy from the audience, but not all of them were the stereotypical villain audiences may have seen on the Elizabethan stage. Even comic actors such as Charles Macklin, as John Russell Brown has argued,[9] played Shylock as a man of fiercely contrasted passions (1741); and in Edmund Kean (1814) audiences could glimpse the terrible fury of a man scorned, credibly human and, in the words of William Hazlitt, "more than half Christian" (*The Chronicle*, 6 March 1816). But the Victorian age marked the most dramatic shift in what the play came to signify. This shift involved an increasing sympathy for Shylock owing to the English sense of cultural enlightenment, a fascination with the exotic "other," and public (if not private) disavowal of institutionalized anti-Semitism which eventually led to Jewish emancipation. The English prided themselves on their tolerance. After centuries of blatant anti-Semitism, Jews, albeit few, were becoming assimilated into the highest ranks of society and were gaining access to political power; a Rothschild was elected to Parliament in 1847, and Benjamin Disraeli became Prime Minister in 1868.

The shift of sentiment in Victorian society is marked by Dickens's radically different portrayals of Jews—from the grotesque caricature Fagin he had drawn in *Oliver Twist* (1837) to his portrait of an emancipated Jew, Riah, in *Our Mutual Friend* (1864). The specter of Shylock as the ur-Jew had hovered over English fiction for years; but it was explicitly challenged by novelists such as Maria Edgeworth, Disraeli himself, and George Eliot, whose *Daniel Deronda* epitomized the view of assimilated Jews as respectable citizens. Reactionary novelists such as Trollope continued to write of "the secret Jew"—the feigned convert to Christianity who, like the "Hebrew Premier" (it was argued), sought to infiltrate and thereby contaminate the Teutonic roots of English society,"[10] but despite such persistent racism, more enlightened views carried the day. Matthew Arnold's *Culture and Anarchy* (1869), a highly influential manifesto for cultural diversity, insisted on the importance of Jews and of "Hebraic" virtues to English national identity and thereby helped to define an English role for the Jew even as it acknowledged—and validated—his otherness.

This change in the conception of Jewishness coincided with an evolving idea of subjectivity: the notion of a coherent self, an individual identity that always amounted to more than the sum of the social roles one played. This new idea of subjectivity, which was evident in the Victorian novel and coincided at the end of the century with theories of the unconscious mind, differed markedly from the Elizabethan notion of personhood as something culturally determined and socially circumscribed. In the nineteenth century, certain of Shakespeare's characters proved to be more susceptible to the concept of subjectivity than others; and these, interestingly, were those on the margins of society, whose identities set them apart from groupings at the hegemonic center of the plays, whose behavior deviated from the norm, and whose marginal status allowed audiences to read motives of opposition, alienation, and subversion into their behavior. It is no coincidence that in our own century, a figure such as Aaron the Moor in *Titus Andronicus* has found increasing favor with audiences. Long condemned as a barbarous blackamoor who practices against the lives of the Roman governing class, he has gained psychological depth as audiences have grown increasingly conscious of racism and its vicious consequences. As an outsider who has learned to assert himself against a corrupt regime, and as a passionate defender of his own individualism and the rights of his illegitimate son, Aaron has acquired a more profound identity attributable to a change in late twentieth-century political consciousness. This process helps to explain, too, why, in the nineteenth century, Hamlet—the prince on the margins of the Danish court, identified as a romantic before his time—became Shakespeare's most coveted tragic role. It also helps to explain why Shylock emerged as a sympathetic victim of social injustice, and why *Merchant* became the most frequently performed of Shakespeare's comedies in the nineteenth century.

Shakespeare's text provided ample evidence for those who, alert to the evils of anti-Semitism, found in Shylock a subjectivity at odds with comic characterization: their new cultural awareness of the "other" intersected with lines that revealed Shylock's sense of alienation. His protest against public humiliation:

> Signor Antonio, many a time and oft
> In the Rialto you have rated me
> About my monies and my usances . . .
> You call me misbeliever, cut-throat dog,
> And spit upon my Jewish gaberdine . . .
>   (1.3.98–104);

his plea for his own humanity in "I am a Jew"; his refusal to abase himself before Christians when they demand to know his reason for revenge—all suggested to Victorians a rich interiority, a pattern of complex psychological responses to his alien status, which made him far more interesting a subject than the Christians.

Choices made by Victorian actors contributed to turning *Merchant* into the tragedy of Shylock. Often act 5 was omitted as too frivolous a reversion to comic romance after the defeat of a great man at trial. The century's most popular Shylock, Henry Irving (who acted the role over a thousand times, beginning in 1879), in a move of telling cultural solipsism, transformed Shylock into an eminent Victorian. "Shakespeare's Jew," Irving claimed, "was . . . not a mere individual . . . [but] a type of the great, grand race . . . a man famous on the Rialto; probably a foremost man in his synagogue—proud of his descent—conscious of his moral superiority to many of the Christians who scoffed at him, and frantic enough, as a religionist, to believe that his vengeance had in it the element of godlike justice."[11] As if to counter theatrical traditions that had persisted through the eighteenth and early nineteenth centuries, Irving protested that "there is nothing in [Shylock's] language, at any time, that indicates the snuffling usurer which some persons regard him, and certainly nothing to justify the use early actors made of the part for the low comedian. He was a religious Jew; learned, for he conducted his case with masterly skillfulness, and his speech is always lofty and full of dignity. Is there a finer language in Shakespeare than Shylock's defence of his race?"[12] Shylock's sentiments, of course, are not always lofty, and some do indeed expose him as a snuffling usurer (though Irving purged the most blatant of them to preserve a decorous image). Most revealing, however, is Irving's celebration of Shylock's "I am a Jew" as a defense of his race. This speech builds inexorably toward Shylock's justification of revenge—a morally questionable end, no matter what the provocation—and in the past it has been delivered as such. But Irving passed over its immediate dramatic function to universalize it as a plea for racial tolerance. Perhaps nothing better indicates the willingness of more enlightened Victorians to redeem the Jew in light of their own cultural values.

Omitting passages that tended to stereotype Shylock, Irving chose instead to foreground those scenes that emphasized his familial bonds and his victimization. Most famously, he interpolated a scene in which Shylock returned home from dining with the Christians to find his daughter fled. According to an eyewitness account, Shylock entered carrying his lantern, crossed the bridge, descended the steps, and crossed stage left to his house. He knocked at the door three times. There was no answer. He paused: the silence disturbed him. With great deliberation he knocked again, three times. Then, "raising his lantern to search the darkened upper windows, across his features came a look of dumb and complete despair."[13] The curtain fell on this picture of "unrelieved simplicity," "the image of the father convulsed with grief."[14]

Later, at the trial, Irving provided a crowd of Jewish onlookers to place Shylock within a sympathetic context, affording him a communal identity as one in a group of dignified patriarchs. Shylock's performance at the trial was heroic, and even in defeat—after his forced conversion—he made a proud exit. Moving toward the door, he was seized with a convulsion and briefly faltered; but he drew himself up to his full height, bent his gaze defiantly on the court and stalked out.[15] This tragedy of the noble Jew victimized by an insular, hypocritical society registered strongly with the public and spawned generations of clones in both Europe and America.

* * *

The history of twentieth-century productions of *Merchant* continued this dichotomy of high and low, of Shylock as vengeful villain or tragic victim, with the play serving as a litmus test of cultural biases. Post-Holocaust productions often added to nineteenth-century traditions the weight of genocide, so that Shylock was made to bear enormous historical significance, anticipating for an audience the horrors that the audience knew lay ahead for Jews. Modern directors adapted the traditions of Irving and his progeny in order to make audiences keenly aware of Shylock's marginal position in a smugly Aryan society: Laurence Olivier alluded explicitly to Irving in his production for the National Theater in 1971, which was set, tellingly, in the late nineteenth century. Irving's strategy, of course, had been to appeal to the pride Victorians took in their enlightened racial tolerance. In young Jonathan Miller, Olivier found a director who was willing to appropriate both Shakespeare's text and Irving's conception of it to demonstrate how the presumably educated Victorians to whom Irving appealed were themselves philistines, their prejudices all the more insidious for being cloaked in shows of courtesy and good will. Miller located the roots of modern prejudice not in religious, but in economic theory and power relations. "Modern anti-Semitism," he argued, "as Hannah Arendt [*The Origins of Totalitarianism*] has shown, has something to do with nineteenth century capitalism and politics rather than with biblical theories about the death of Christ." Jewish financiers often provided the capital with which industrialists made their fortunes, but such provision did not guarantee them access to power or social privilege. In fact, Jews came to be blamed for exploitation, unemployment, market fluctuations, and other economic woes for which capitalists had no ready solutions. Miller used Shakespeare's text to develop such themes: he set Shylock "within the context of the Rothschilds Banking House, which found that great wealth and prestige never meant exemption from the hatred and anti-Semitism of European society—whose rapid economic and political expansion the Rothschilds were helping to finance."[16]

What particularly interested Miller were not overt differences between Christians and Jews, but the ways in which ethnic groups "look for appearances which will substantiate their prejudices." He therefore envisaged a Shylock not exotically different from the gentiles, but socially and culturally assimilated:

> Allowing Shylock to appear as one among many businessmen, scarcely distinguishable from them . . . made sense of his claim that, apart from his customs, a Jew is like everyone else. . . . I felt that there was no need in a nineteenth century setting to distinguish him except by the customs and rituals that he follows discreetly in his home. This highlights and emphasizes the absurdity of the racial prejudice.[17]

Updating the play thus served Miller's agenda as readily as an anthropologically correct production had served Irving's: each director sought thereby to discover the origins of his own culture's attitudes toward Jews, and both suppressed the play's comic potential in order to present the "real"—that is, the tragically verisimilar—Shylock as representative of his whole persecuted race.

Olivier seized the opportunity to give Shylock as much psychological depth as he had to the tragic heroes he had played, paying careful attention to the subtle ways in which aliens learn to cope in a hostile environment, just as Irving had done a hundred years earlier. Yet unlike Irving, whose model was a Levantine patriarch, Olivier conceived Shylock as a Victorian Jew, a banker striving for assimilation but not yet in command of the manners or noblesse oblige of a

Rothschild. Driven by a first-generation desire for social respectability, his Shylock paradoxically emulates those very gentiles he abhors. He dresses like them, only better. Wearing a black frock coat over black striped trousers, carrying a silver-topped walking stick and a newspaper from which he reads current market prices through a golden pince-nez—"then let me see, the rate" (1.3.96)—he is every inch the financier. Only the yarmulke hidden by his top hat identifies him as an outsider.

To ensure that audiences recognized the distinction, Miller manipulated the text to Shylock's advantage, cutting such obviously prejudicial passages as "I did dream of money bags tonight" (2.5.18), Shylock's vindictive aside about Antonio in 1.3, and the whole of 2.8 in which Salerio and Solanio mock Shylock for wailing over the loss of his ducats and his daughter. The Victorian gentility for which Miller strove made these adjustments not only permissible, but necessary: Shylock in this period would not admit to hating Antonio because he is a Christian, or because he lends out money gratis, any more than Antonio would spit on Shylock in public or kick him over his threshold. The bond for a pound of flesh thus becomes not a ruse to mask a deeper malice as it was for Irving, but a means by which Shylock strives to win the acceptance of the gentiles by playing according to their rules. It is a joke by which Shylock shows the Christians that he, too, can lend money free of interest. Miller revises Shakespeare's text most startlingly when he suggests that Shylock's revenge occurs to him for the first time in act 3: it is motivated not by an implacable hatred of Christians, but by the loss of Jessica, and by this alone.

Other directors in the twentieth century have used *Merchant* to serve their own political agendas. Most conspicuously, in Hitler's Germany, where some directors felt uncomfortable enough with the play to omit it from their repertoires, others reshaped it to comply with Third Reich propaganda: they staged it as farce or commedia, with Shylock sporting a red wig and false nose and gloating over his money bags, and with the interracial marriage between Jessica and Lorenzo discreetly omitted. There were fifty such productions of *Merchant* in Germany between 1933 and 1944.[18] German directors, however, were not alone in reviving this ostensibly Elizabethan tradition: similar productions were popular throughout the 1930s in England (even at the Stratford Festival), Russia and Eastern Europe, and they attested to the desire of audiences, suffering through the worst economic depression in modern history, to find in Shylock a scapegoat for their own misery, to laugh at the Jew as a comic butt and thus give vent to a rising anti-Semitic feeling without having to acknowledge it.

Postwar directors have had a dialogue with these productions as well, in ways that have made audiences explicitly aware of historical contexts and the ways in which art may advance a political agenda. Beginning (interestingly) with German director Georg Tabori, and followed by directors in America and elsewhere, productions have revived *Merchant* as commedia only to frame it as a play-within-a-play performed by Jewish inmates at a concentration camp, for the delight of the commandant and his officers.[19] This framing device radically alters viewers' responses to the performance of the play as comedy; they are made keenly aware of the subject positions of the actor-inmates who are forced to participate in their own degradation. Despite what they see in the performance of the play itself, audiences view Shylock not as the villain of tradition, but as a victim—an inmate undergoing an excruciating self-annihilation for the entertainment of philistine murderers. Such productions invest audiences with a double historical consciousness: of the play as an anti-Semitic comedy, and of the propagandistic use to which that play was put to justify the extermination of Jews. Such double consciousness results in a fascinating reversal of conventional responses, for every anti-Semitic trick that provokes mirth among the stage audiences of Nazis causes the theater audience to wince in pain; farce turns to tragedy; and the ironies compel the audience to meditate on the horrific uses to which Shakespeare historically has been put.

* * *

Today, however, anti-Semitism is no longer the burning issue it was earlier this century. A post-Holocaust sensibility is largely taken for granted. Nearly every time a major theater company announces a production of *Merchant*, Jewish groups weigh in to ensure that the play's anti-Semitism will be historically contextualized; once-radical productions now seem conventional; and the insistent focus on Shylock as Jew has become a bit old hat. Postmodern directors have begun to use Shylock as a free-floating signifier for other sorts of discrimination: Peter Sellars, for instance, in his controversial production of 1994 set in Venice Beach, California, cast Shylock and the other Jews as African Americans, caught in the cultural and economic wars waged against them by both Latinos (the Venetians) and

Asian Americans (the Belmontese).[20] Productions such as this are a sign that in America, at least, anti-Semitism hasn't the cultural currency it once had, and that its force is being translated into terms of more contemporary social unrest.

Yet other productions in the late twentieth century have directed their gaze elsewhere, to characters whose subject positions were less interesting to earlier generations: sometimes to Portia, whose plight as a daughter bound by the will of her father challenges contemporary beliefs about the rights of women; but more often to the merchant himself, Antonio. The reasons for this scrutiny of Antonio are worth examining. Traditionally, he has been played as a mercantile prince of the new order, willing to sacrifice all he has for the sake of friendship: his love for Bassanio suggests fraternal affection, a chivalric virtue idealized in Renaissance literature; and as for his enigmatic sadness which opens the play—"In sooth I know not why I am so sad" (1.1.1)—it may be sixteenth-century melancholy, or twentieth-century depression, or simply the loneliness of a successful business man. There is not much to suggest a rich inner life; and until recently, his potential for subjectivity aroused little curiosity. Yet certain lines, certain behaviors, remain puzzling, insufficiently explained by this traditional account of his character. In the opening scene, for example, he too adamantly rejects his friends' speculation that he is in love with "Fie, fie!" (1.1.47). Later, Salerio describes in unusually emotional terms Bassanio's leave-taking, wherein Antonio, his "eye being big with tears, / Turning his face, . . . put his hand behind him, / And with affection wondrous sensible"—a phrase denoting physical amity—"He wrung Bassanio's hand" (2.8.47–50). The tender passion conveyed in this description elicits Solanio's reply, "I think he only loves the world for him" (51). Later, arrested for nonpayment of the bond, Antonio writes to Bassanio in Belmont, informing him of his misfortune and bribing him to return to Venice: "if your love do not persuade you to come, let not my letter" (3.2.318–19). And at the trial, he utters parting lines to Bassanio which sound oddly like a challenge:

> Commend me to your honourable wife.
> Tell her the process of Antonio's end,
> Say how I loved you, speak me fair in death,
> And when the tale is told, bid her be judge
> Whether Bassanio had not once a love.
> (4.1.269–73)

These lines suggest an implicit rivalry between Antonio and Portia that Bassanio only exacerbates by replying that life itself, his wife, and all the world are not esteemed above Antonio.

To read more than generous friendship into these lines may be anachronistic; yet for audiences who understand love as a term of romance rather than mere friendship, for critics with a psychoanalytic bent, and in societies where homosocial bonding sometimes elides seamlessly into homosexual practice, interpreting Antonio as a gay man suffering an unrequited love for Bassanio makes sense. The fact that homosexuality is now out of the closet—that gay rights are a topic of political debate, that representations of homosexuality are common, and that queer theory has found a niche in academe—has legitimated the identification of Antonio as a figure whose alienation from the play's main characters may now be understood as repressed homosexual longing. Political change, therefore, and the opening of a new cultural discourse have altered audiences to a potential subjectivity for Antonio that would not have been available to audiences in the early modern period, when homosexuality as an identity was not understood as it is today and when homosexual acts were punished as sodomy; or to audiences in the nineteenth century, when homosexuality was labeled effeminacy—a mode of deviant behavior—and homosexual acts, gross indecency.[21] Today, Shakespeare's text may be freely heard to resonate with homosexual overtones: "My purse, my person, my extremest means/ Lie all unlocked to your occasions," Antonio urges Bassanio, the homophonic play on "purse" and "person" binding body and money together in his offer (1.1.137–38). "I am a tainted wether of the flock,/ Meetest for death," he tells Bassanio at trial; "the weakest kind of fruit/ Drops earliest to the ground, and so let me" (4.1.114–16). Lines such as these are now heard to betray Antonio's assimilation of society's homophobia and to reveal a sense of his own marginalization. Such positioning explains his behavior in new ways—as a product of repression, self-loathing, even anger against the dominant heterosexist culture.[22]

Although Antonio's love for Bassanio was identified as homosexual as early as 1963, when W. H. Auden wrote about it in *The Dyer's Hand*, playing Antonio as a gay man has moved center stage only since the 1970s.[23] This movement has coincided with a relaxation of laws which criminalized homosexual behavior and forbid the discussion—let alone representation—of homosexuality on stage. As

Nicholas de Jongh reminds us, in 1958 Britain's Lord Chamberlain relaxed his absolute veto upon the discussion of homosexuality on stage. The Obscene Publications Acts of 1959 and 1964, which roughly offered the equivalent test of "redeeming social value" in the U.S., laid the foundations for legalizing homosexual acts between consenting adult males; but not until the passing of the Theaters Act of 1968, which abolished the Lord Chamberlain's theatrical powers altogether and gave the stage safeguards similar to those provided for "obscene publications," was the ban on representing homosexuality on stage lifted. A similarly permissive spirit prevailed in the U.S. and in 1965 New York State lifted its ban upon the depiction of homosexuality in the theater.[24] Thus gay plays began to find mainstream audiences: in London, Joe Orton's *Entertaining Mister Sloane* in 1964; in New York, Martin Crowley's *The Boys in the Band*, 1968.

The Royal Shakespeare Company (RSC), while not openly courting revisionist gay Shakespeare, nevertheless began to let homosexual subtexts out of the closet, so that of its 1971 production of *Merchant*, Judi Dench could claim that her Portia felt a neurotic rivalry with Antonio for the love of Bassanio, which drove her to despair during the trial scene. Tony Church, who played Antonio in this production, reported to me that the contest between Portia and Antonio over the ring that Portia has made Bassanio vow never to remove from his finger was regarded as pivotal to their conception of the play. In her disguise as the doctor of laws, Portia has asked for the ring as payment for legal services, but Bassanio has refused. When, moments later, Gratiano overtakes her with the ring, she suspects that Antonio has bent Bassanio to his will. And she's right; for after she leaves the court unpaid, Antonio implores his friend,

> My lord Bassanio, let him have the ring.
> Let his deservings and my love withal
> Be valued 'gainst your wife's commandement.
> (4.1.445–47)

The return to Belmont, usually characterized by comic banter and romantic closure, proved otherwise in this production. To test her suspicion of Antonio's emotional hold over her husband, Portia chides Bassanio for being unfaithful, hoping to smoke out Antonio. She succeeds. Antonio's admission, "I am th'unhappy subject of these quarrels" (5.1.238), proves her suspicion warranted. If Dench's

Portia was distressed to find a homosexual rival in Antonio, however, critics seemed not to notice it: indeed, this production was praised for its affirmation of the play's romantic values. Only Murray Biggs, writing in *Shakespeare Survey* the following year, remarked on its undercurrent of sexual rivalry, and did so disapprovingly, calling it a violation of Shakespeare's text.[25]

By 1987, however, an RSC production directed by Bill Alexander used Antonio's homosexuality as an overt metaphor for social alienation: understood in the context of the AIDS crisis generally, and AIDS plays more specifically (a number of which had run in London), Alexander's production made explicitly homosexual what heretofore had been latent. Comments by no fewer than fifteen reviewers attest to its importance. Antonio is "a solidly middle-aged homosexual," according to Frank Rich (*New York Times*, 16 June 1987), "a man hopelessly in love with Bassanio" (*Sunday Telegraph*, 23 May 1987), "a repressed homosexual" (*Time Out*, 6 May 1987), and a "tormented closet gay" (*Guardian*, 1 May 1987) whose "homosexual passion" for Bassanio is "touchingly signaled" in the opening scene (*Daily Telegraph*, 29 April 1988). Critics couldn't help revealing their cultural biases toward homosexuality. Bassanio, for playing on the older man's love, was condemned as a "bisexual opportunist" (*The Listener*, 14 May 1987) who "appears to exist on the instincts of a successful rent boy" (*Daily Mail*, 30 April 1987).

But however judgmental and possibly homophobic, the accusations are not altogether unfounded. When Bassanio speaks of coming freshly off from his debts, confiding "To you, Antonio,/ I owe the most in money and in love" (1.1.129–30), he lays one hand casually on Antonio's shoulder, the other on his chest, fingering his ruffled collar. In response, Antonio places both hands on Bassanio's shoulders, leaving them there just a moment too long to signify mere friendship. When Bassanio begins to sing Portia's praises, Antonio turns away from him; but Bassanio knows how to overcome such body language. On "O my Antonio, had I but the means" (172), he approaches his seated benefactor from behind, goes down on one knee and places a hand on his shoulder; when Antonio, jealously unmoved, says he cannot raise the present sum, Bassanio moves his right arm around Antonio's waist. That does the trick. On "therefore, go forth,/ Try what my credit can in Venice do" (178–79), Antonio rises to embrace Bassanio; and before they release each other, he plants a kiss, full and frank, on Bassanio's lips. Bassanio steps back, surprised but not offended, as indeed he should not be: his behavior has provoked that kiss.

Responses to this scene reveal as much about the critics—and their gender—as about the scene itself. Noting "the passion of Antonio's kiss," Martin Hoyle in the *Financial Times* commented that the overtly homosexual bias of the production brought to mind "Germaine Greer's recent remarks on the basic homosexuality of the English" (27 April 1988). If Hoyle's response was self-consciously and even defensively male (note how he takes these men as his countrymen, not even pretending to see them as Venetian), Mary Harron approached the scene with Portia's concerns in mind. Remarking that Bassanio was "presented more blatantly than usual as Antonio's former lover," she wrote in *The Observer* that "there is much sexual tension and pathos in the opening scene between these two, creating a thread of suspense every time Portia sees them together, as we wonder—how much does she know?" (3 May 1987). Attempting critical objectivity, Paul Taylor of *The Independent* protested that homosexuality precluded a "straight" reading of the text (his word); for, he asked, how can Christian magnanimity be taken seriously "if Antonio's generous funding of Bassanio's wife-hunting is over-played as the selfish stratagem by which a depressed homosexual manages to keep an emotional hold over—and wrest a few impassioned kisses from—the friend he is bound to lose?" (28 April 1988). How, indeed?

By the winter of 1998–99, in Andrei Serban's modern-dress production for the American Repertory Theater in Cambridge, Antonio had clearly become the character in whose marginal status the director was most interested: an unfulfilled gay man whose inner torment the audience was encouraged to probe even as Shylock performed a comic schtick that made him far less sympathetic, and even, according to some, villainous. That audiences had come to accept Antonio as a homosexual is demonstrated by the fact that his relationship with Bassanio drew little critical comment. Serban, a Romanian director noted for his provocative cultural politics, turned Venice into "a decadent and sexually ambiguous world" according to the reviewer for *The New York Times*, and the play itself into a gay fantasia. Antonio appears as a self-absorbed middle-aged man, urbane and restless: to him enter Salerio and Solanio, customarily played as younger sycophants, but here as a couple of aging queens—dandily dressed, flamboyantly gay—the roles taken by two of the best senior actors in the company, Jeremy Geidt and Stephen Rowe. As they grill Antonio about his sadness, it becomes clear that they have a long history with him; and when Solanio taunts him with "Why then, you are in love" (1.1.46), he playfully bestrides one of the palli, the striped poles used to moor gondolas, riding and stroking it like an outsized phallus. These men laugh comfortably with one another—a clearly established circle of friends—and thereby suggest a gay subculture in which individuals share a political identity. When Bassanio enters to ask for a loan, he cannot help but know how Antonio feels; and lest we miss the point, Antonio places a hand on Bassanio's knee when he bids him to "say to me what I should do . . . And I am prest unto it" (157–59), but withdraws it when Bassanio rises to intone—in an embarrassed attempt to clarify his sexual orientation—"In Belmont is a lady richly left" (160).

The discomfort Judi Dench admitted to feeling over Bassanio's indebtedness to Antonio is, in this production, played full throttle. Belmont, act 3: to the newly affianced lovers, Salerio enters with a letter to Bassanio from Antonio. Portia registers suspicion at the flamboyance of the messenger and curiosity about the message itself, which has come to her husband from a "good friend" (3.2.232). When Bassanio reports, at her insistence, how deeply indebted he is to Antonio, Portia grows visibly uncomfortable; and when the others have left, and she presses him to read the letter aloud, the dynamic between the two lovers is prickly. All the phrasing of the letter can be heard, as Portia apparently hears it, as code from a male lover: "Sweet Bassanio . . . my bond to the Jew is forfeit, and since in paying it, it is impossible I should live, all debts are cleared between you and I if I might but see you at my death." Portia might even suspect emotional blackmail in the final lines: "Notwithstanding, use your pleasure; if your love do not persuade you to come, let not my letter" (314–19)—for at this, she sinks down on a bench, clutching her stomach in distress. Historians might object that Portia's understanding of the "love" between her husband and his friend is anachronistic, but it makes her motive for journeying to Venice more ambiguous than a simple desire to save the day. Here, in disguise, she may be motivated by a desire to see her rival for Bassanio's love, and to spy on them undetected.

The trial scene capitalizes on this sexual tension. A grief-stricken Bassanio clings to Antonio; Antonio's admission that he is a tainted wether of the flock is spoken privately to Bassanio, thus strengthening the homosexual nuance; and his barely contained desire to reveal his true feelings to Bassanio in "bid [your wife] be judge/ Whether Bassanio had not once a love" is met with an equally passionate protestation by Bassanio that he would sacrifice even his wife to save Antonio's life. This exchange plays as an emotional confession by two male lovers: whether Bassanio means what he says or is simply saying what he thinks Antonio wants to hear, is moot. All possibilities are potent; and Portia's response, so often delivered comically—"Your wife would give you little thanks for that/ If she were by to hear" (284–85)—here is spoken as an anguished aside. Such anguish may prompt Portia to bring Antonio to the brink of death before producing the comic quibble that spares him: Serban leaves unresolved whether her discovery that the bond permits "no jot of blood" (302) is a sudden inspiration or a calculated delay. Thirty years ago, Judi Dench's speculation that Portia was torn between love for her husband and a desire to punish him owing to sexual jealousy seemed startling. Today, it seems tame: our culture has evolved (one might say coarsened) to the point where, in performance, jealousy needs visibly to sicken Portia when she begins to suspect her husband's fidelity, and her rivalry with Antonio needs to be explicitly signaled at the trial.[26]

Act 5—once notorious for trivializing the tragedy of Shylock with its banter about rings—comes into its own in this production. In a staging that reinforces Portia's heteronormative authority, Serban uses the banter to contain the threatened homosexual disruption of the play's romantic closure. Antonio remains a hesitant onlooker as Portia taunts Bassanio about his fidelity, she clearly suspicious, as was Judi Dench, that Antonio had persuaded her husband to give up the ring. When at last he is moved to defend Bassanio—"I dare be bound again,/ My soul upon the forfeit, that your lord/ Will never more break faith advisedly" (5.1.251–53)—Portia seizes the occasion to assert her power over the two men. Enjoining Antonio to "Give him this [ring],/ And bid him keep it better than the other" (254–55), she recreates, as if in jest but with full command, the love triangle that had earlier brought her to despair. Portia and Antonio stand flanking the seated Bassanio. She hands the ring to Antonio, who then, under her controlling gaze, places it on Bassanio's finger. The moment resonates with cultural significance: by Portia's permission, Antonio enacts a kind of wedding ritual with Bassanio, the import of which is that Antonio will ensure that Bassanio will remain true to her. A host of associations crowds an audience's reception of the scene: traditional wedding rituals, the current debate over gay marriages, assertions of women's rights in marriage, and the tyranny of heteronormative values. Such associations help to construct the play's cultural significance; for Serban's shaping of *Merchant* as the tragedy of Antonio wrests authority from Shakespeare's text and demonstrates how complicit the audience, the performers, and the historical moment are in determining a play's meaning. At the conclusion of this production, after the lovers have filed out, Antonio is joined by a masked Shylock. They circle one another in a dumb show, paired in their alienation. The critic of *The Boston Globe* saw this as a mirror image: the two men "both trapped by their identities, paralyzed by the disguises they are forced to wear." I read it as an emblem of how Antonio has now come to rival, if not displace, Shylock as the site of the play's most contested political meaning.

I am not suggesting that this is a right or a wrong reading of the play: theoretical accounts of performance do not make such judgments. Rather, I provide this account to demonstrate how the study of social and political contexts can prove particularly useful to performance critics. It helps them to understand how performances have shaped plays for audiences at different moments in history, to analyze how theater practitioners and audiences collaborate to invest a play with significance and to give it meaning at a specific place and time. By looking at performance through the lenses of theory, we can begin to understand more fully the cultural work theater does.

Notes

1. De Marinis, Marco. 1987. "Dramaturgy of the Spectator." Translated by Paul Dwyer. *The Drama Review* 31, no. 2: 100.

2. Jordan, Thomas. 1664. "The Forfeiture." In *The Royal Arbor of Loyal Poesie* (1664).

3. All quotations are from Mahood, M. M., ed. 1987. *The Merchant of Venice*. New Cambridge edition, Cambridge: Cambridge University Press.

4. James Shapiro discussed the history of the Marranos and Conversos, the vexed question of what constituted a "Jew" in early-modern England, and the myths that grew up around London's Jewish community in the first two chapters of Shapiro, James. 1996. *Shakespeare and the Jews*. New York: Columbia University Press, 13–88.

5. Sanders, Wilbur. 1968. *The Dramatist and the Received Idea*. Cambridge: Cambridge University Press, 345–46. See also Sinsheimer, Hermann. 1947. *Shylock: The History of a Character or the Myth of the Jew*.

6. Moisan, Thomas. 1987. "'Which Is the Merchant Here? And Which the Jew?': Subversion and Recuperation in *The Merchant of Venice*." In *Shakespeare Reproduced:*

The Text in History and Ideology, edited by Jean E. Howard and Marion F. O'Connor. 189.

7. Draper, John W. 1935. "Usury in *The Merchant of Venice.*" *Modern Philology* 33: 39–45.

8. Girard, Rene. "'To Entrap the Wisest': A Reading of *The Merchant of Venice.*" In *Literature and Society, Selected Papers from the English Institute,* edited by Edward Said. Baltimore, 100–119.

9. Brown, John Russell, ed. 1955. *The Merchant of Venice,* New Arden Series. London, xxxii. For a more complete account of the play's early stage history, see Brown. 1961. "The Realization of Shylock." In *Early Shakespeare.* Stratford-upon-Avon Studies 3. London, 187–209.

10. The most comprehensive study of the Jew in nineteenth-century fiction is Ragussis, Michael. 1995. *Figures of Conversion: The Jewish Question and English National Identity.* Durham, NC: Duke University Press, see especially ch. 2 on "Patronizing Shylock," ch. 5 on the "Hebrew Premier," and ch. 6 on "The Secret Jew in England." For further study of Eliot, Trollope, and Arnold, see ch. 2 of Cheyette, Bryan. 1993. *Constructions of "The Jew" in English Literature and Society: Racial Representations, 1875–1945.* Cambridge: Cambridge University Press.

11. Hatton, Joseph. 1884. *Henry Irving's Impressions of America.* Vol. 1. London, 269.

12. Ibid., 266.

13. *Critical Notes on Shylock as Played by Sir Henry Irving.* British Theater Museum, n.d.

14. Lelyveld, Toby. 1960. *Shylock on the Stage.* Cleveland, 85–86; William Winter. 1885. *Henry Irving.* New York, 182.

15. See the extended account of this scene in Irving, Laurence. 1951. *Henry Irving: The Actor and His World.* London, 343–44.

16. "Director Interview: Jonathan Miller Talks to Peter Ansorge." *Plays and Players* 17, no. 6: 52–53, 59.

17. Miller, Jonathan. 1986. *Subsequent Performances.* London, 155–56.

18. Wulf, Josef. [1966] 1983. *Theater und Film im Dritten Reich.* Reprint. Berlin and Vienna, 280–83. Wilhelm Hortmann traces the drop in number of productions of *The Merchant* in Germany during the Third Reich—from an average of twenty to thirty per year (two hundred performances) prior to 1933, to less than one-third that total after 1933—in Hortmann, Wilhelm. 1998. *Shakespeare on the German Stage: The Twentieth Century.* Cambridge: Cambridge University Press, 134–36.

19. For comments on Tabori's production for the Williamstown (Massachusetts) Festival in 1966, see Shapiro, Michael. 1986. "Shylock the Jew Onstage: Past and Present." *Shofar* (Winter): 1–11. Tabori restaged *The Merchant* in Munich to even more potent effect in 1978; and his concentration camp setting has been borrowed for numerous American college productions, notably at the University of Iowa and at California State Polytechnic University.

20. See Worthen, William. 1997. *Shakespeare and the Authority of Performance.* Cambridge: Cambridge University Press, 76–94.

21. Among recent studies of homosexuality and its representation in the early modern period, perhaps the most influential have been Bray, Alan. 1982. *Homosexuality in Renaissance England.* London: Gay Men's Press; Smith, Bruce R. 1991. *Homosexual Desire in Shakespeare's England: A Cultural Poetics.* Chicago: University of Chicago

Press; Goldberg, Jonathan, ed. 1994. *Queering the Renaissance*. Durham, NC: Duke University Press; DiGangi, Mario. 1997. *The Homoerotics of Early Modern Drama*. Cambridge: Cambridge University Press; and Masten, Jeffrey. 1997. *Textual Intercourse: Collaboration, Authorship, and Sexualities in Renaissance Drama*. Cambridge: Cambridge University Press.

22. Alan Sinfield addresses the reasons for, and resistance to, seeing Antonio as homosexual in Sinfield, Alan. 1991. "How to Read *The Merchant of Venice* Without Being Heterosexist." *Alternative Shakespeares* 2, edited by Terence Hawkes. London: Routledge, 122–39. Readings of Antonio's unrequited homoerotic love for Bassanio have proliferated in recent years: see, for example, Geary, Keith. 1984. "The Nature of Portia's Victory: Turning to Men in *The Merchant of Venice*." *Shakespeare Survey 37*: 55–68; Kleinberg, Seymour. 1983. "*The Merchant of Venice*: The Homosexual as Anti-Semite in Nascent Capitalism." In *Literary Visions of Homosexuality*, edited by Stuart Kellogg. New York: Haworth Press, 113–26; Pequigney, Joseph. 1992. "The Two Antonios and Same-Sex Love in *Twelfth Night* and *The Merchant of Venice*." *English Literary Renaissance* 22: 201–21; and Patterson, Steve. "The Bankruptcy of Homoerotic Amity in Shakespeare's *Merchant of Venice*." *Shakespeare Quarterly 50* (Spring: 9–32).

23. Auden, W. H. 1963. "Brothers and Others." In *The Dyer's Hand*. London: Faber.

24. de Jongh, Nicholas. 1992. *Not in Front of the Audience: Homosexuality On Stage*. London: Routledge, 89–90.

25. Biggs, Murray. 1972. "A Neurotic Portia." *Shakespeare Survey 25*: 153–59. Two years after this production, Ellis Rabb staged *The Merchant* at Lincoln Center with a similar bias: a homosexual relationship between Antonio and Bassanio corrosively affected Bassanio's marriage to Portia who, as a sophisticated older woman, was keenly aware that her young husband was bound to another man, and whose game with rings in act 5 underscored her suspicion. Unlike reviewers for Hands's production, however, reviewers of this production were attentive to its sexual politics, though not necessarily sympathetic. According to the *Christian Science Monitor* (5 March 1973), even the trial scene was "twisted to serve the bisexual romantic triangulation imposed on the text."

26. The review of this production by Cook, Dorothy, and Wayne Cook. 1999. *Shakespeare Bulletin 17* (Spring): 8–9; astutely points out Antonio's stereotypically homosexual mannerisms, a Bassanio "confused by his bisexuality," and a Portia who, after reading Antonio's letter, "was compelled to wonder . . . whether she had made a terrible mistake."

The Merchant of Venice

Ralph Berry

The central issue confronting the director of *The Merchant of Venice* is the catastrophe of our century, the Holocaust. How far can our consciousness of this catastrophe impinge upon, or dominate, a contemporary production? On the one hand is a director's decision to play up the Star of David aspects with set and costume. On the other is the view, as Patrick Stewart puts it, that "these passages of anti-Semitic expression in *The Merchant* will reverberate powerfully for any audience in this second half of the twentieth century. Actor and director will not need to emphasize them, nor must they be avoided."[1] There is here not so much a line to be crossed, as a shifting territory where matters can be got across with, or without, a megaphone.

That said, it's impossible not to feel some sympathy with David Nathan, drama critic of the *Jewish Chronicle* (London). Having reviewed eight productions of *Merchant* within a few years, he wrote: "I have had enough of this damned play." It is "deeply offensive, no matter how it is done."[2] But the play is there to be done, remains popular when done, and requires strategic decisions to be taken by the director.

The main emphasis has to be decided early. Jonathan Miller, whose *Merchant* (first at the National, then on TV) is I think much the best version available on video, set his production in the Venice of the late nineteenth century. He had a number of contingent reasons, but centrally: "I did not want to set it in a modern era where all the twentieth century notions of Anti-Semitism would overwhelm the play."[3] The Count of Primoli's photographs of Venice in the 1880s gave Miller his cue, with scenes set in the red plush of Florian's café in the Piazza San Marco. That was as late as Miller preferred to go.

There is naturally a fundamentalist position, that Renaissance Venice is the only one that counts. It is expounded vigorously by Bill Alexander, who directed a well-praised *Merchant* (with Anthony Sher as Shylock) in 1987. He set it in the Jacobean period, about thirty years after the play's date of composition:

> I was convinced that *The Merchant of Venice* had to be set in the Jacobean period, because I am convinced that you cannot do that play unless you understand the cruelty of the world, the society in which it was written. All the themes of the play—justice, mercy, the law, revenge, money, love and how they relate to all those things—are thrown off centre if you try to find an analogical social context. And central to that is the notion of justice, and what justice meant to the Elizabethans and Jacobeans, in physical terms. Their direct experience of justice was that if you transgressed you were likely to end up with your head on the Bridge—or, in the case of the Venetian traitor, buried upside down in the pavement with your feet sticking up, or hanged, drawn, and quartered. Those were the realities of punishment.

If, says Alexander, you put Shylock's revenge in a Victorian or twentieth-century context, there's an immediate suspension of credibility. And apart from that,

> the casual cruelty of the world . . . is partly what motivates Shylock's desire for revenge, the world in which he is treated with a casual humiliation, the hypocrisy of the role of the Jews in seventeenth century Venice. They were there in order to lend money to the Christians, because the law forbade Christians to lend money to each other. And therefore, they couldn't finance their capital ventures any other way than by having people prepared to lend money. The whole of the social context is vital to unleashing the themes of the play.[4]

That argument is very strong. Personally, I'm no kind of purist against modernized Shakespeare. I fall easily for *The Two Gentlemen of Verona* where Speed plays the chauffeur. But the *Merchant* is too hard, too real for that: I think there is always a part of our minds that refuses to be switched off, that says "Look, in the Victorian era the law didn't permit private citizens to cut chunks out of other citizens' flesh in a civil suit." In its own terms Alexander's argument is irrefutable.

He also implies a design point that directors keep in mind: the Elizabethan era is hopeless in terms of literal fashion. All those balloon pants and farthingales just don't work on stage. Now if you move on two or three decades from 1596, the date of *The Merchant of Venice*, you can keep Renaissance values while discarding the wrong kind of gear. Clothes changed. We can see that the Puritan Fathers are in some vestigial ways our fashion ancestors, while Essex and Leicester belong to prehistory. Jacobean, for Alexander, means the very beginning of modern times, the times we can relate to, just as it retains the values of Renaissance Venice.

But let's leave on deck some kind of large choice, ancient or modern, and look at how they throw up problems and opportunities. I want now to look at three recent productions, each of which offers a different way into the *Merchant*. The direct application of modern history, twentieth-century European history to the *Merchant* is possible and has been done. In 1991 Tim Luscombe directed a *Merchant* for the English Shakespeare Company. The agenda for this company has always been broadly populist. Its premier director, Michael Bogdanov, wants above all to relate the concerns of a Shakespeare play to today's world.

Luscombe's approach to the *Merchant* seemed logical enough, in terms both of play and of company. He chose a historical analogue, setting the play in the Italy of the 1930s. Specifically, the program dated this *Merchant* to 1938, and set out a history lesson on the rise of anti-Semitism in Fascist Italy. "Hence Luscombe could show more and more Venetians wearing Fascist uniforms as the play progressed, and could follow Lorenzo's flight with Jessica (2.6) with a scene of an elderly Jew beaten up by blackshirted thugs."[5]

So what is wrong with this? As Peter Holland shows (in his *English Shakespeares*), the historical analogue breaks down as soon as you start to examine it. Holland cites Jonathan Steinberg's book *All or Nothing* (1990) to show that "Italian Fascism was decisively lacking in anti-Semitism and its government resisted Nazi pressure to hand over its Jewish community."[6] "If the analogy is not historically true," says Holland, "it serves no purpose."[7] It doesn't even work within the play: would Shylock have got a fair hearing from the authorities in 1938? On his legal claim to kill an Aryan?

The problems go on. If the Venetians are Fascists, then Shylock is shorn of any villainy. Indeed, this production did everything it could to place Shylock in the best possible light. As Holland mordantly puts it, "The modern anxiety of presenting a bad Jew was soothed; Shylock became a decent chap, a businessman with barely a hint of Jewish accent, seen at first working efficiently at his desk"[8] And when the spectator emotions turned against Shylock and his huge carving knife during the trial scene, "The audience found itself siding with the Fascists."[9] I really think that this *Merchant* need not detain us long. One conclusion seems clear. You don't solve the problems of this play by dragging it into modern times. Jonathan Miller's reservation is well advised.

I have a lot more time for another approach via the contemporary though, David Thacker's *Merchant* for the RSC in 1993. On Thacker's view, the dominant theme is money. Indeed, Michael Billington of the *Guardian* wrote that Thacker had "chosen to make money the protagonist." (5 June 1993) This *Merchant* was set in the City of London during the 1980s, in one of those temples of finance whose atmosphere closely resembles a cathedral. People wear Armani suits and talk into cordless phones, while computers flash up green figures. Steel and glass frame the atrium. At the same time the set becomes a wine bar, where the younger sort of executives celebrate the day's trading with champagne before taking off for their Porsches. This, as several commentators noted, is the world of Gordon Gekko. When Launcelot Gobbo, the office tea boy, speaks of "Black Monday" (2.5.24) he is clearly referring to one of those fabled disaster days that strike the market.[10] Venice, in short, has become "a yuppified City of London."[11]

David Calder played Shylock as a highly civilized banker, who goes home to listen to Schubert on his CD player. Billington thought that "In this closed financial community David Calder's uneasily assimilated Shylock is clearly a prosperous outsider tolerated for his expertise." (*Guardian*, 5 June 1993) On this showing, Shylock *became* a Jew after the shock of Jessica's desertion. "The villainy you teach me I will execute" is the key line, thought Alistair Macaulay of the *Financial Times* (5 June 1993). This Shylock donned a skullcap in the trial scene, after being indistinguishable from any other businessman. He may perhaps have taken his cue from Olivier, to whom Kenneth Tynan wrote:

> The man at the beginning of the play is a businessman first and foremost, only secondarily a Jew. When the Christians steal his daughter, he begins to realize what it means to be Jewish, and by the end of the trial he knows it through and through.[12]

Of course, you can't push the City too hard upon the text. The *Daily Telegraph* reviewer found that it held up for about a quarter of an hour. To raise just one point: if the play is about money, has not the City long since given up debating whether taking interest is a good thing or not? I'd judge that the sheer opulence of the set, plus the ingratiating detail of current analogues, kept the production as an engaging and lively fable. After all, the *Merchant* is largely about the intricate processes and subtle power of wealth. Even so, the most seasoned reviewers were skeptical. For Benedict Nightingale of the *Times*, "But the approach brings with it more problems than gains" (7 June 1993). And Paul Taylor (*Independent*, 8 June 1993) felt that "Attempts to update *The Merchant of Venice* are almost always bound to run into snags and contradictions." I would respectfully delete "almost."

A third way into *The Merchant of Venice* is to go back to Renaissance Venice. This approach handles the problems rather well, and is much more resourceful than one might at first think. It is certainly much more than narrowly historicist.

The rationale for a Renaissance setting is trenchantly put by Gregory Doran. He played Solanio in Alexander's *Merchant* (1987), and while he liked a good deal in that production he had his reservations. When the time came for him to direct the play (RSC, 1997), he made public his view. The Alexander production, he believed,

> loaded the play in the post-Holocaust sense. It overbalanced it. The casket scenes went for nothing, but they are crucial because it is all about human values—Portia is a commodity, too.
>
> The play has been hijacked by history. We are putting it back into the world of Renaissance trade. We've started with the title: Shylock was a merchant of Venice. I wanted to take the swastikas and stars of David out of the play.[13]

There are, I believe, two sorts of positive reasons for setting the play in Renaissance Venice. One is cultural, the other topographical. I'll start with topography, which has a greater bearing on the play than is generally realized.

Shakespeare, it is clear, knew a great deal about Venice. It is not one of his fantasy locations, like Navarre or Illyria or Bohemia. Venice is real. Whether from Emilia Bassano, if she was indeed his mistress, or from travelers to Italy, he picked up some vital information (more of it in *Othello*). Shakespeare does not, it is true, go in for the Baedeker name dropping of Ben Jonson:

> I, your Scoto Mantuano, who was ever wont to fix my bank in face of the public Piazza, near the shelter of the Portico to the Procuratia...
> (*Volpone*, 2.2.34–36)

Jonson is showing off, of course, as usual. But Shakespeare knows his way around Venice too. The Rialto is mentioned several times, not as the bridge which it is today but as the exchange where "gentlemen and merchants" do business together. This exchange is the center of news gathering, and the key line is "What news on the Rialto?" The line is repeated (1.3.34, 3.1.1), always a sign that Shakespeare attaches importance to the point. Shylock shares the line with Solanio. The Rialto is the nerve center of Venice.

That perennial adjunct to Venetian life, the gondola, gets a mention (2.2.8), in a context that explains its meaning fully. Above all, Shakespeare expounds a word which is never mentioned in the text but which dominates the play. It is ghetto.

This aspect of the matter is still architecturally visible, the quarter where Jews lived in Venice. The word "ghetto" actually originated in Venice, where the first one came into existence. "Getto" means "foundry," and it applied to the site of the first ghetto in Venice. In 1516 the senate decided that all Jews in Venice should move to the Ghetto Nuovo, an urban islet with two access points that could be closed at night. This arrangement enabled the authorities to protect the Jews from violence and looting, and to impose an effective curfew upon them. The Venetian authorities were relatively lenient toward the Jews by European standards. But they laid down a policy that combined protection and separation.

So *ghetto* symbolized the segregation of Jews in Venice, and gradually became a generic name used all over Europe. (And now used loosely to denote any quarter where a given group, including diplomats, lives together.) Today in Venice one can visit the Ghetto Vecchio and Ghetto Novissima, and still feel the impress of architecture on the mind. Since the area for building was fixed and could not be expanded, the buildings had to reach up to the sky. They are tall for Venice, growing to six or more stories. The windows tend to face inward toward the square or open areas, not outward to the rest of Venice. "The Ghetto turned a blind face to the City," wrote Mary McCarthy in *Venice Observed*.[14] The overall effect of the Jewish quarter is austere, closed-off, inward-looking, not without a sense of danger.

This is what caught the imagination of a distinguished Shylock, Ian McDiarmid. He played the role for the Royal Shakespeare Company in 1984, and tells of his preparations:

> Before rehearsals began, I went to Venice, where I had a wonderful time and found one thing of use. In the Jewish Quarter, Ghetto Nuovo, I was fascinated to see that all the windows looked inward towards the square. None looked outward to the city and the sea beyond. So, I extrapolated,

the Jew was not permitted to look outwards. He had no alternative but to look inwards. Light was shut out. He was left obsessively to contemplate the dark. Less metaphorically, inside were his possessions. His house was itself, and also the sole repository of his property: his wealth ("the means whereby I live") and his daughter, Jessica ("the prop/That doth sustain my house"). Shylock's wealth and his daughter represented his internal life, "ducats and my daughter!" and his "precious, precious jewels!". When they were stolen by the Christians, I conjectured, it was as if his identity and his heart had been removed at one stroke, his inside ripped out. At hand, to assuage the agony, was a sure provider of short-term relief—revenge.[15]

That insight explains a great deal in *The Merchant of Venice*, especially the meaning of "house"—for "Ghetto" does not appear. House and land are security itself. Shylock's distrust of the sea comes out early, "and then there is the peril of waters, winds and rocks" (1.3.20). McDiarmid also accounts for Shylock's distaste for Christian intruders into the ghetto streets:

> What, are there masques? Hear you me, Jessica:
> Lock up my doors; and when you hear the drum
> And the vile squealing of the wry necked fife,
> Clamber not you up to the casements then,
> Nor thrust your head into the public street
> To gaze on Christian fools with varnished faces;
> But stop my house's ears—I mean my casements . . .
> (2.5.27–33)

This is historically quite correct. Christian revelers often took part in masques and street dancing in the Jewish quarter during the feast of Purim. To Shylock they are intruders, disturbers of his peace of mind. And the eternal solace? It is the synagogue, still there. "Go Tubal, and meet me at our synagogue, go, good Tubal, at our synagogue, Tubal." (3.1.102–3)

When I reread this passage I was struck with the force of the possessive pronoun. One might say casually "the synagogue"; Shylock says "our synagogue," and repeats it. He's reminding Tubal of another bond, their common membership of the Jewish community.

Tubal is one of the key tests of an intelligent production of the *Merchant*. He is emphatically not a civilian spear carrier, an actor's alternative to the Salad parts. Tubal is the sketch for a Jewish chorus. In him can be seen the attitude of the Jewish community toward Shylock.

I never saw him better played than by Raymond Westwell, absolutely magnetic in his scene with Patrick Stewart's Shylock. Westwell, as he passed across the table his receipts from the Genoa Hilton, was markedly reserved and detached. The Jewish community, he implied, would be supportive of Shylock, but thought its own thoughts as to the advisability of his conduct.

Peter Holland is illuminating on the role of Tubal in Thacker's production.

> Thacker increased Tubal's presence in the play. He was on stage in 1.3 when Bassanio and Antonio came to borrow the money from Shylock. David Calder really did not have the 3,000 ducats available (1.3.51–54) and Tubal's whispered offer solved the problem: "Tubal, a wealthy Hebrew of my tribe, Will furnish me" (55–56). Skull-capped from the start, offering advice about Shylock's biblical analogy to Jacob like a resident rabbinical scholar, Nick Simons' Tubal increasingly marked his distance from Shylock's maniacal pursuit of Antonio. When Shylock announced "I will have the heart of him if he forfeit" (3.1.117–18), he put his hand firmly on an open book, a prayer book I presume, on his desk and Tubal registered horror at this abuse of religion. In Shylock's confrontation with Salerio and Solanio . . . Tubal made clear his total rejection of Shylock's course of action, a response underlined by placing the interval here as Shylock and Tubal exited in different directions. It was an unspoken plea from Tubal that drew from Shylock the acerbic "Tell not me of mercy" (3.3.1) as Antonio was going to jail. At the trial scene, while Antonio was backed by his friends, Shylock was conspicuously alone, the seats behind him empty.[16]

The stage direction for the general entrance to the trial scene does not name Tubal. Tubal is our bridge between the topography of Venice, the synagogue, and the cultural values that sustain the play. I cite one of those highly condensed, tight passages where Shakespeare is concerned to get a lot across in a short space. Following the flight of Jessica with Lorenzo, reports Solanio,

> The villain Jew with outcries raised the Duke,
> Who went with him to search Bassanio's ship.
> He came too late—the ship was under sail,
> But there the Duke was given to understand
> That in a gondola was seen together
> Lorenzo and his amorous Jessica.
> Besides, Antonio certified the Duke
> They were not with Bassanio on his ship.
> (2.8.4–11)

The gondola is the symbol of illicit love, as well as a picturesque detail in the scene. It is placed in a context of relationships and assumptions. Shylock has clout with the authorities. He may be socially undesirable, but he is too wealthy and important to be ignored. The Duke is put to considerable inconvenience in investigating Shylock's complaint, but essentially accepts Shylock's point of view, that elopements are bad and should be stopped.

What is the relationship between Shylock and the Duke (Doge), the civic leader? Since Venice is founded on wealth, it follows that the sanctity of money and contracts is the basic law. The main plot of *The Merchant of Venice* turns on the enforcement of a contract. Antonio plays the futures market and gets hit, badly. He has neither hedged nor diversified, just doubled up. He is well liked and the Duke does what he can to help. But a contract is a contract. As we saw recently in Singapore, a city-state founded on commerce is absolutely committed to the law of contract—and to punishing malefactors who bring into disrepute the city's high standards. Shylock is a leading representative of Venice's financial community, and an indispensable source of credit to the state. He has to be taken seriously.

All these considerations feed into a Renaissance setting, and this is what Gregory Doran chose. The reviewers had no doubt where they stood.

> Doran's *Merchant* is firmly rooted in historical time and space. This is the Venice of Shakespeare's day, where Jews and Christians deal with each other without making much effort to hide their mutual disgust, while still admitting that they are collaborators in the business of getting and spending. (James Treadwell, *The Spectator*, 20 December 1997)

Doran "puts the play back into the sixteenth century," thought Alistair Macaulay (*Financial Times*, 15 December 1997). And the *Daily Express* critic states that references to the Holocaust and Star of David were banished (21 December 1997).

The set designer can, of course, keep the canals, gondolas, Piazza San Marco and the Rialto for Renaissance Venice. It is much more than a designer's cliché. Moreover, the historical Venice comes into view at other points. Doran, when playing Solanio in Alexander's production, records this discovery.

> We decided to . . . explore the seedy, decadent underbelly of the world of Venice which they inhabit and which Bassanio, away from it all in Belmont,

comes to realize is all "outward show." In researching the period I discovered that the young Henry III of France had visited Venice on his way back from Cracow, where as a young general he had won the throne of Poland. When he returned from Venice, however, he was a different man. The court was stupefied to see him caked in powder, hung with precious stones, and surrounded by a flock of parrots and little dogs. He began to hold fêtes in the royal parks, decked out in a pink damask dress embroidered with pearls, emerald pendants in his ears, diamonds in his hair, and his beard dyed with violet powder. Such was the civilizing effect of La Serenissima.[17]

Here too there are resources for those directors who wish to return to the Renaissance.

The main drift of all this is clear. There is, I believe, a very strong case for recapturing the essential ambivalence of *The Merchant of Venice*. This is achieved by returning the play to its historical origins, a Venice where the uneasy collaboration of Christians and Jews offers something to all parties. John Gross says, rightly, that *The Merchant of Venice*, though not an anti-Semitic play, is a major document in the history of anti-Semitism.[18] It is all of that and much more too. Let those two titles entered at the Stationers' Register, *The Merchant of Venice* and *The Jew of Venice*, stand cipher for the ambivalence of the piece.

Notes

Citations are to Mahood, M. M., ed. 1987. *The Merchant of Venice*. New Cambridge Shakespeare Edition. Cambridge: Cambridge University Press.

1. Stewart, Patrick. 1985. "Shylock." In *Players of Shakespeare 1*, edited by Philip Brockbank. Cambridge: Cambridge University Press, 19.
2. *Jewish Chronicle* (London). 1997. 26 December.
3. Miller, Jonathan. 1986. *Subsequent Performances*. London: Faber & Faber, 107.
4. Alexander, Bill. 1989. Interview. In *On Directing Shakespeare: Interviews with Contemporary Directors*, by Ralph Berry. Second edition. London: Hamish Hamilton, 181–82.
5. Holland, Peter. 1997. *English Shakespeares*. Cambridge: Cambridge University Press, 95.
6. Ibid.
7. Ibid.
8. Ibid.
9. Ibid.
10. Arditti, Michael. 1993. *Evening Standard*. 4 June.

11. Luscombe, Christopher. 1998. "Launcelot Gobbo in *The Merchant of Venice* with Moth in *Love's Labour's Lost.*" In *Players of Shakespeare 4*, edited by Robert Smallwood. Cambridge: Cambridge University Press, 20.

12. Tynan, Kenneth. 1994. *Letters.* Edited by Kathleen Tynan. London: Weidenfeld & Nicolson, 472.

13. Quoted by Neill, Heather. 1992. "Shylock's Pounded Flesh." *The Times*, 9 December.

14. McCarthy, Mary. *Venice Observed.*

15. McDiarmid, Ian. 1988. "Shylock in *The Merchant of Venice.*" In *Players of Shakespeare 2*, edited by Russell Jackson and Robert Smallwood. Cambridge: Cambridge University Press, 48.

16. Holland, 1997, 164.

17. Doran, Gregory. 1993. "Solanio in *The Merchant of Venice.*" In *Players of Shakespeare 3*, edited by Russell Jackson and Robert Smallwood. Cambridge: Cambridge University Press, 71.

18. Gross, John. 1992. *Shylock.* London: Chatto & Windus, 326. "It is still a masterpiece, but there is a permanent chill in the air, even in the garden of Belmont." (326) For the latest thinking on Venice as it appeared in the age of Shakespeare, see Mulryne, J. R. "History and Myth in *The Merchant of Venice.*" And Salinger, Leo. 1993. "The Idea of Venice in Shakespeare and Ben Jonson." In *Shakespeare's Italy: Functions of Italian Locations in Renaissance Drama*, edited by Michele Marrapodi, A. J. Hoenselaars, Marcello Capuzzo, and L. Falzon Santucci. Manchester: Manchester University Press.

Romeo and Juliet in Performance

Jay L. Halio

Thanks to Tom Stoppard, now we know how *Romeo and Juliet* was written, though I can't believe that the original title was *Romeo and Ethel, the Pirate's Daughter.* Thanks to *Shakespeare in Love,* we also know how and when a woman first graced the Elizabethan stage. Joking aside, and forgiving a number of historical inaccuracies—or shall we say, creative license?—this excellent movie really says a good deal about Shakespeare's early theater and about theater generally. It is a popular and welcome counterweight to modern scholarly edited texts, which tend to "freeze" Shakespeare's plays in a way that would amaze the dramatist, were he alive to see them, and that amazes contemporary theatrical directors and producers, who take liberties comparable to Stoppard's when staging any of Shakespeare's plays. Far more interested in putting on a good show for their audiences, wherever they are, than in reproducing what we sometimes call "museum Shakespeare," these theater professionals know what Shakespeare knew and what poor old Henslowe, as Stoppard represents him in the film, knew only too well: you have to stage a good "get penny" if you want to stay in business.

Academics, of course, once we have tenure, don't worry so much about staying in business as we seek the "authentic" Shakespearean text. But does such a thing exist? And if it does, what is it? I shall be arguing here that there is more than one authentic text for *Romeo and Juliet*—two at least, but probably more—as there are for many of Shakespeare's plays, such as *Hamlet* and *King Lear,* to cite just two others whose early editions exist in more than one version. Often these versions reflect literary manuscripts, as in the second quartos of *Romeo and Juliet* and *Hamlet,* and alternative acting versions, as in the first quartos of these plays or the Folio text of *King Lear.* From this kind of evidence, it does not take a rocket scientist to deduce that Shakespeare's plays, like those of his—or our—contemporaries, were never "fixed," as modern editions seem to suggest. They were adapted for performance, often undergoing revisions that included selections, rewritten passages, and sometimes additions to the original manuscript document. These revisions might occur during rehearsals or later for revivals or at almost any time during the play's stage life.[1] The play's the thing, after all, or the playscript, as I shall call it here—not the "text," or the modern edited version, although many playscripts are—quite rightly—based upon those texts, as for example the Royal Shakespeare Company's prompt books reveal.[2]

* * *

This, then, is my starting point. I have argued elsewhere that the first printed version of *Romeo and Juliet* (Q1) is not a pirated or corrupt reconstruction of the play but an authentic acting version of it, based upon the author's manuscript, which it adapts and seriously shortens.[3] When writing *Romeo and Juliet,* Shakespeare was in his so-called lyric phase—the phase that includes *King Richard II* and *A Midsummer Night's Dream* and the last act of *The Merchant of Venice.* During this period (whether he was or was not in love with a woman masquerading as a boy actor) he was clearly given to flights of fancy that issued forth in some excellent lyric poetry. But lyric poetry is not dramatic poetry. Shakespeare realized this as his career progressed, learning to fuse the requirements of drama with the impulse to poetic expression. In a late play, such as *Macbeth,* he integrated drama and poetry as no other dramatist has ever done. If we can judge from the second quarto of *Romeo and Juliet,* the manuscript when presented to the acting company was too long. Several drastic cuts were made, resulting in something closer to the first quarto version. But unlike Q1 *Hamlet,* which involves far different problems and questions, the original structure of *Romeo and Juliet* was preserved. What chiefly happened was that long speeches, such as Juliet's invocation to night in act 3, scene 2, were severely cut, but no scenes were omitted, like act 4, scene 3 in the Folio *King Lear.* Interestingly, Mercutio's Queen Mab speech was not cut but rather clarified from the error-prone version found in the longer second quarto. Why that speech, which contributes little or nothing to the dramatic action, should be retained and others not, I'm not sure; but as we examine later acting versions of the play, let's see what happens to this famous speech, long a favorite with audiences—and with actors, too, whether Burbage or someone else played the part.

For those unacquainted with theatrical practice in the seventeenth century, it may come as a surprise that in some representations of the play Romeo and Juliet did not die at the end. The transformation of Shakespeare's tragedy into a tragicomedy was accomplished by James Howard. Shortly thereafter Thomas Otway rewrote the play and renamed it *The Rise and Fall of Caius Marius,* performed by the Duke's Men in 1679. Combining Roman intrigue with Elizabethan tragedy, Otway drastically altered Shakespeare's work even more than Shakespeare altered Brooke's poem. To judge from its frequent revivals—it held the stage until 1735—and its several editions (1680 to 1703)—Otway's redaction apparently suited the tastes of the time, which was not Shakespeare's time any more than our time is.

What Otway did was, after all, what Shakespeare and his contemporaries did with other old plays. He rewrote *Romeo and Juliet,* or adapted it, just as today we sometimes adapt plays—more often than not into musicals, like *West Side Story.* At least Otway did not call the play by Shakespeare's title (whether Marlowe suggested it to Shakespeare or not). That is perhaps the first and best clue to an adaptation as opposed to an interpretation. Here I shall be concerned not with adaptations, fascinating though they often are, but with interpretations; that is, with the playscript *Romeo and Juliet* as it has been variously presented over the centuries.

* * *

Skipping past James Howard's tragicomedy, which is more of an adaptation than an interpretation, I will begin with eighteenth-century productions, notorious though they are for severely revising Shakespeare's original. A good starting place is David Garrick's versions of the play.[4] Colley Cibber had already begun the process of restoring Shakespeare's original, a process that Garrick continued; nevertheless, we would not quite recognize in any of Garrick's versions the play as Shakespeare wrote it. Gone are Lady Montague's role, Romeo's infatuation with Rosaline, and much of the original dialogue. The most notable difference, however, is Juliet's funeral procession, which Garrick added in 1750. This includes several airs, or dirges, written for the play with their own musical accompaniment. Even more startling to modern audiences is the revised ending. Garrick occasionally rewrote Shakespeare's lines; here he interpolated about sixty-five new ones. Juliet awakens before Romeo dies, but after he has already taken the poison that will kill him. They engage in an emotionally fraught dialogue, reasserting their eternal love, and then Romeo dies. Juliet faints, overcome by shock, as Friar Lawrence enters. When she revives, Friar Lawrence tries to get her to leave with him, as in Shakespeare's text, but to no avail. She sends him away, takes Romeo's dagger, and stabs herself.

That's where Garrick's version ends—with Juliet's death. No denouement, no catharsis, such as we find in the received text: Garrick knew Juliet's death would make a good final curtain. His contemporaries and immediate successors certainly agreed: this ending, as Garrick rewrote it, held the stage for the next hundred years. Elsewhere Garrick made numerous cuts and revisions, shortening the play, removing bawdry, and generally fashioning the play more to his century's taste than to Shakespeare's. For example, though he kept Mercutio's Queen Mab speech, he eliminated the last half dozen lines, which describe the way Mab treats young women. Not until the twentieth century were these lines again spoken from the stage. The dialogue between Peter and the musicians at the end of 3.5 is gone, since it also violated eighteenth-century notions of decorum. Like Q1, Garrick's text shortened Juliet's invocation to night and in other passages reduced or eliminated Shakespeare's exuberant lyricism or Friar Lawrence's tendency to long-winded exhortations. Sensibly, Garrick also curtailed the weeping and wailing when the family discover Juliet's body in 4.5. Garrick explains what he has done and why he has done it in his "Advertisement," or preface, to the 1763 edition of the play.

John Philip Kemble's acting edition succeeded Garrick's but retained most of the latter's innovations. The American actor, Charlotte Cushman, was responsible for removing most of them—what she called "flummery"—and further restored what Shakespeare wrote in her London production of 1845. But her script also reveals many cuts, mostly for shortening and for maintaining the Victorian sense of propriety. Hence, a good deal of the bawdry is still missing along with such episodes as Peter and the musicians. Most of the ending of 3.1 is gone, too, as superfluous, since the audience, if not the prince, already knows what has happened in the fight scenes. She followed Garrick and Q1 in shortening Juliet's invocation to night, but she eliminated the funeral procession at the beginning of act 5 and restored the contours of Shakespeare's ending, while at the same time shortening it. Cutting Shakespeare's original text became even more necessary now, when time was needed for scene shifting on the Victorian stage. An uncut *Romeo and Juliet* was simply not feasible then any more than it seems to have been on Shakespeare's stage.[5]

These days we have become accustomed to seeing women enact roles usually or naturally reserved for men, such as Puck in *A Midsummer Night's Dream* or the Fool in *King Lear*. Sarah Bernhardt played Hamlet toward the end of her career, and more recently Diane Venora did the same at New York's Public Theater. Not long ago, Fiona Shaw played Richard II. But when Charlotte Cushman played Romeo against her sister Susan's Juliet, she created something of a sensation. Why? She was not the first woman to assay the role; more than a dozen others had done so before her in America as Ellen Tree had in London.[6] Moreover, many women had acted in breeches roles, not only as Rosalind and Viola, but also as Richard III, Shylock, and even Falstaff, not to mention non-Shakespearean roles such as Sir Henry Wildair in *The Constant Couple*, Sir Peter Teazle, and other male characters.[7] Cushman's Romeo, therefore, was by no means unprecedented. What was unprecedented was the way she played the role, with a passion unequaled by any woman—or man. Her biographer, Joseph Leach, describes her as:

> an impetuous youth afire with love for Juliet. Her Romeo's love-sick speeches to Friar Lawrence rang completely true. His supple gestures, his leaps over the garden walls, his impassioned words, the flash of his sword driving at the "Furious Tybalt" carried such conviction that few in the audience remembered that a woman's skill lay behind them.[8]

When they did remember who it was, and that her sister Susan was Juliet, the object of such passion, some in the audience, especially when they appeared together in Scotland, became visibly disturbed.[9] Nevertheless, Cushman's *Romeo and Juliet* triumphed on the Victorian stage as well as over Shakespeare's "improvers."

Until Cushman revitalized *Romeo and Juliet*, the play had grown less popular than it was in Garrick's day, when he and Spranger Barry vied with each other as Romeo at Covent Garden and Drury Lane. Although Charles Kemble, Edmund Kean, Macready, and others enacted Romeo, none had endowed the role with the imaginative and emotional power it requires. After Cushman's success, the play once more gained favor. But Cushman's success was limited: she shaped the play into a star vehicle, eliminating or reducing Shakespeare's emphasis on the lovers as a pair. Or as Jill Levenson puts it, "Whereas Garrick made both lovers central and uniformly pathetic . . . Cushman elicited from Shakespeare's contrarieties the vision of one protagonist who experiences passion so intensely that he finally dies of it" (1987, 34). It remained for others to restore the dual passion of Romeo *and* Juliet to Shakespeare's original.

In 1882 Henry Irving, at the age of forty-four, played Romeo at the Lyceum Theater in London. His was a lavish production, in the manner of late Victorian pictorial extravaganzas, but his representation of the tragic hero again lacked fire. His failure derived in part from the well known problem the role involves: "When a man has achieved the experience requisite to *act* Romeo, he has ceased to be young enough to *look* it; and this discrepancy is felt to be unendurable in the young, passionate Romeo."[10] In 1881 at the age of twenty-eight Johnston Forbes-Robertson began playing Romeo opposite Helen Modjeska, but it was not until more than ten years later, in America with Mary Anderson, that he reached the heights of his portrayal.[11] Unlike Irving, what he lost in youth, he had gained in "authority and poetic fervour."[12]

If Romeo seems to have dominated these nineteenth-century productions, what happened to Juliet? Her role, as a careful analysis shows, is equally important—some would say even more important, as she grows to a maturity greater, perhaps, than her lover's. The problem seems to be that the actors cast in her role were not quite up to the mark. True, Cushman had arranged the text to emphasize the part of Romeo, and her sister Susan, while competent, could not match Charlotte's brilliance. However effective Ellen Terry was in Irving's production in the first half of the play, she became much less so in the later, tragic passages. Mrs. Patrick Campbell's representation in Forbes-Robertson's production suffered similarly, though it was her first time in the part.[13] Another American actor, California-born Mary Anderson, seems to be the only Juliet during this period to have won acclaim. George Odell maintains that her production of *Romeo and Juliet* was the best he ever saw.[14]

Odell's opinion is confirmed—surpassed, rather—by William Winter, who says he saw Anderson perform as Juliet some thirty-five times over twelve years, or from her first attempts at the role when she was merely sixteen, to her triumphs later in London and New York. "In its maturity," he says,

> Miss Anderson's performance of Juliet was one of intrinsic charm, superlative beauty of artistic form, and great energy of passion and power of pathos; and, more than that . . . it was saturated with the force and color

of *tragedy*. Her performance was notably exceptional in the felicity with which she harmonized the discordant elements in Juliet,—the combination of inexperienced, sweet, and winning girlishness with a woman's capacity to love and suffer. The felicity of her artistic method was particularly exhibited in the discriminative skill with which she marked the change from girl to woman.[15]

* * *

What, then, does all this historical information teach us? Of what use is it today to know how *Romeo and Juliet* was staged in previous centuries? Well, for one thing, it shows that actors, directors, producers are constantly trying to render Shakespeare's plays in ways that speak directly to their audiences. In the nineteenth century, producers understood the interest of their age in historical accuracy, at least as regards the stage settings of the plays; they therefore went to considerable lengths to reproduce Verona as they thought, after serious scholarly investigation, Verona must have looked in the sixteenth century. This was no concern in Shakespeare's day or in the seventeenth and eighteenth centuries, when the actors dressed in the fashion of their own times. Today, we sometimes see modern dress productions and productions in Elizabethan settings. Which is preferable? And what happens when Shakespeare's play is transformed to another medium—opera, ballet, or film?

Let's take the first question first: modern dress or Elizabethan setting.[16] In 1986 the Royal Shakespeare Company performed *Romeo and Juliet* in present-day Verona, complete with swimming pool, camcorders (for the final scene, staged as a media event), and even an Alfa-Romeo sports car driven onto the set. Michael Bogdanov directed and, as he always does, insisted on bringing Shakespeare up to date. Hence the cast resembled many contemporary types: teenage gang members, Italian business tycoons, socially ambitious wives, bored young men and women straight out of *La Dolce Vita*. Of course, in transposing time frames, Bogdanov had to make certain adjustments: switchblade knives replaced rapiers, and Romeo killed himself with an overdose of drugs administered by a hypodermic needle. These are incidentals, after all.[17] Although the script was cut—hardly a surprise, as we have seen—the dialogue was not otherwise seriously altered, and no funeral procession was added, although golden statues of Romeo and Juliet were on view during the concluding media event.[18]

That is the point, the main one, it seems to me—preserving as much as possible of Shakespeare's language. Not all of it is essential, as the 1597 quarto (Q1) demonstrates. We need not genuflect, as some pedants do, before Shakespeare's oeuvre and insist on preserving every last word in performance.[19] Shakespeare knew that some passages might prove expendable, and producers through the centuries have known it, as I have indicated. But "translating" Shakespeare into modern verse, or worse, is something else again. No one would defend these days what Garrick did to *Romeo and Juliet* in act 5, when he had Romeo and Juliet engage in dialogue after Romeo swallowed his fatal draught. True, when deletions of the script are made, some bridging of the text needs to be done, and a careful splice becomes necessary. John Barton, for example, is adept at doing that, as he proved when the RSC performed the *Henry VI* plays in the 1960s. And occasionally an archaic term needs a modern synonym. But that's all. Audiences today can follow quite well, thank you, Shakespeare's dialogue, as the evidence from Ashland, Oregon, and many other Shakespeare festivals around the country demonstrate every year. Their actors perform before thousands of spectators, not all of whom are Shakespeare scholars; many may never have even read the playscript beforehand.

Key to Shakespearean performance, whether it is *Romeo and Juliet* or some other play, is not the setting, which should probably be kept as simple as possible to avoid the excesses of "designer theater" (Ralph Berry's term). No, the key is interpretation, and here is where shaping the playscript can exercise a decided if sometimes subtle influence, as Charlotte Cushman's script showed. How important are Mercutio and the nurse? By reducing their roles, eighteenth- and nineteenth-century producers distorted Shakespeare's original, removing from it much of the earthy aspect of human love that contrasts with Romeo and Juliet's experience but is also a part of it. Again, what happens when, as Garrick did, you eliminate references to Rosaline and omit or muzzle Romeo's Petrarchan love lines? An important dimension of the play gets lost. But is every line that Friar Lawrence speaks necessary? Can't his lengthier speeches be shortened without similar distortions? I think they can, and so do many directors, past and present, who curtail the worthy friar's verbosity. Again, does every conceit in Romeo's or Juliet's love lyrics have to be preserved, or can a staging of the play dispense with some, though not all, of them?

These are the kinds of questions that staging *Romeo and Juliet*—and many other plays—involves. But prior to all of them is the vexed issue of directorial concept. At what point does the overall interpretation of the play—the one that helps determine the size and shape of the playscript but also the interpretation of roles, the set design, stage business, and much else—come into being? Some directors fix their concepts before their actors are even cast; in fact, the concept may determine who will play what role. In 1960 Franco Zeffirelli, directing the play for the Old Vic in London, determined from the outset to emphasize the play as a young person's tragedy, which of course it is; therefore, he used young actors for his principal leads, casting John Stride and Judi Dench as the young lovers. It was a good choice, though when it came to his film version, Olivia Hussey and Leonard Whiting did not have the training or the experience that such roles require, and spectacle more than acting dominated the production—inevitably, perhaps, given the medium of film. Recently, a production in Israel used a multiethnic cast to highlight contemporary conflicts—Israelis versus Arabs as Montagues and Capulets.[20] Similarly, in January 1999 a student production at the University of Virginia, concerned with racism on and off campus, cast white actors as Montagues and blacks as Capulets.[21] Are such transpositions not only of time and place but of ethnicity legitimate? While on the one hand they tend to localize the conflicts inherent in the play, on the other they also universalize them as they make them more specific; indeed, by making them specific they encourage universalization.[22]

A production's scenography is only one way of addressing—or dressing up—the play's Shakespearean "meanings," and not the most important. Modern dress settings are ultimately a superficial means of coming to grips with a play in an attempt to "make it new." If we believe with Ben Jonson that Shakespeare's plays were not of an age but for all time, then "making it new" really means revitalizing our experience in such a way that we see and feel and understand Shakespeare's plays as contemporary artifacts speaking directly to us. That, I need not add, is more easily said than done, but that is precisely the director's and the actors' job. Or, as William Worthen puts it:

> Despite the radical discontinuities between Shakespeare, his theater, his culture, and the circumstances of the modern stage, the modern director stages an authentic encounter with Shakespeare, transcending the differences of history, culture, language, theater. The "director" creates a modern timeless "Shakespeare." (1997, 54)

Worthen goes on to argue that the director's task is, then, essentially to find a "modern idiom" for the play, such as Jonathan Miller did in his BBC-TV production of *The Taming of the Shrew* with John Cleese as Petruchio (58). The director's task must be accomplished without wholesale violence to the play's genre, structure, and underlying myths, which careful analysis of the playscript can provide. "Merely using the full or original or authentic text of a play," Worthen continues, "is in itself no guarantee of fidelity" (61), which his analysis of Peter Sellars's 1994 *Merchant of Venice* demonstrates (76–94). Shaping the playscript, as Shakespeare's company did and as the first quarto of *Romeo and Juliet* reveals, to find and deliver its "modern idiom" is all to the purpose, which is to convey "a sense of the spirit or meaning of the play that transcends the concrete accidents of any particular version of the text."[23]

* * *

What I have been arguing throughout this paper, using *Romeo and Juliet* as an example, is for reconsideration of the concept of authenticity as a criterion for Shakespearean performance. In his important book, *Shakespeare and the Authority of Performance,* William Worthen has aptly discussed the issue, and much of my argument (as my references indicate) relies upon some of those he puts forward, though more eloquently and at greater length. At the risk of oversimplifying his position, let me agree that the authenticity, or "authority," of a performance is by no means so closely identified as it may seem with the printed texts of Shakespeare's plays, which themselves involve questions of authenticity. While Worthen does not review eighteenth and nineteenth century productions and prompt books in detail as I have done, he knows what they signify for us today. Citing Philip McGuire's earlier work in *Speechless Dialect* and studies by other competent scholars, he notes how the increasing availability of printed texts and the concomitant literacy of audiences in the eighteenth century and later have affected our notions of dramatic authenticity, as has the rise of "English literature." "Performance had an independent tradition," he says (28), and this tradition—I second his claim—needs to be recovered, analyzed, and understood. Increasingly today, thanks to the growing abundance of performance criticism, which includes detailed reviews of Shakespearean productions such as *Shakespeare Bulletin* publishes several times a year, the tradition of performance has begun to reassert itself among scholars. This is decidedly not to say that editions, as "authentic" as modern scholars can make them, are irrelevant to the appraisal of Shakespeare's plays in performance. Shakespeare's language is still primary. But it is not the single or sole reference point for understanding "Shakespeare." It is where we begin, necessarily, and it is where we must return where productions of his plays are concerned. Literary analysis and theatrical analysis have, or should have, a symbiotic relation to each other. In the best scholarship and criticism, as in the best performances, they always do.

Notes

1. For a fuller discussion of this matter, specifically as it relates to *King Lear*, see the textual introduction to Halio, Jay L. New Cambridge Shakespeare edition of that play. Compare Marcus, Leah. 1988. *Puzzling Shakespeare: Local Reading and Its Discontents.* Berkeley: University of California Press, 44: "Nothing we know about the conditions of production in the Renaissance playhouse allows us to hope for single authoritative versions of the plays." See also the account of what happens when a play is produced as regards the use of more than one text in determining the script for a given production in Worthen, W. B. 1997. *Shakespeare and the Authority of Performance.* Cambridge: Cambridge University Press, 23. Worthen concludes, cogently: "Each Shakespeare performance is an independent *production* of the work, part of an emerging series of texts/performances rather than a restatement or return to a single source."

2. Worthen, 1997, 6, cites Roland Barthes's useful description of the "epistemological slide" in the conception of written texts, from "the traditional notion of the *work*" to the more relativized sense of the *text*. Heath, Stephen. 1988. "From Work to Text." In *Image—Music—Text*, edited and translated by Stephen Heath. New York: Farrar, Straus and Giroux, 155–56.

3. See "Handy-Dandy: Q1/Q2 *Romeo and Juliet*." 1995. In *Shakespeare's* Romeo and Juliet: *Texts, Contexts, and Interpretation.* Newark: University of Delaware Press, 123–50.

4. The plural is deliberate, since Garrick, like many other actor-managers in his time, revised the playscript from time to time over the course of a quarter century during which it had many revivals. My references are to Garrick's 1763 acting edition, although many of his alterations date back to his first acting edition of 1750. He first produced the play in 1748.

5. Whether Cushman or her manager at London's Haymarket Theater, Benjamin Webster, deserves credit for the restoration of much of Shakespeare's text is not certain. See Levenson, Jill. 1987. *Shakespeare in Performance: Romeo and Juliet.* Manchester: Manchester University Press, 32–35, who gives a succinct but penetrating analysis of Cushman's achievement.

6. Ibid., 32. Levenson cites Yeater, James Willis. 1959. "Charlotte Cushman, American Actress." Ph.D. diss., University of Illinois, 117.

7. See Price, W. T. 1894. *A Life of Charlotte Cushman.* New York: Brentano's, 121–28.

8. Leach, Joseph. 1970. *Bright Particular Star.* New Haven: Yale University Press, 65. For some contemporary accounts of the Cushmans' performance, see Stebbins, Emma. 1878. *Charlotte Cushman: Her Letters and Memories of Her Life.* Boston: Houghton, Osgood, 1878, 60–63; Leach 1970, 175–76, and Levenson 1987, 38–40. Stebbins attributes Charlotte's desire to support her sister in the demanding role of Juliet as one reason for her decision to play Romeo. On the other hand, for Cushman, as Leach argues, "Romeo was more than a role." In it "she could vent a level of emotion that she recognized more and more as basic to her own nature" (1878, 171).

9. Leach 1970, 169–70. As Leach notes, Charles and Fanny Kemble, father and daughter, had played Romeo and Juliet on occasion without arousing objections, but that was not quite the same thing.

10. Stebbins 1878, 59. Zeffirelli and Lurhman both faced this problem in their film versions of the play when they cast young and relatively inexperienced actors in the major roles, with what success, see below.

11. See Winter, William. 1915. *Shakespeare on the Stage*, second series. New York: Moffat, Yard, 136.

12. Odell, George C. D. 1920. *Shakespeare from Betterton to Irving.* 2 vols. New York: Scribner's, 2:389. Forbes-Robertson used Irving's edition, which had become standard for productions of *Romeo and Juliet* since 1882. Irving had shortened the play: he eliminated dialogue that would offend Victorian sensibilities—hence Mercutio's role is severely cut as well as the nurse's monologue in 1.3—and omitted in essential matters, such as many of Friar Lawrence's lines, part of Juliet's invocation to night, everything in 3.1 after Romeo's exit, all of 4.2, 4.4, and much of 4.5, especially the episode between Peter and the musicians. Like Cushman, he did not include Garrick's funeral procession at the beginning of act 5 or Juliet's awakening before Romeo dies. But he did cut everything after Juliet's death except for Prince Escalus's last four lines.

13. Winter, 1915. 137.

14. Odell, George C. D. 1927–49. *Annals of the New York Stage.* 15 vols. New York: Columbia University Press, 13.20. Compare his comments also in Odell 1920, 2:381, 434–35.

15. Winter, 1915, 276–78. In this chapter on Anderson as Juliet in Winter, William. 1886. *The Stage Life of Mary Anderson.* New York: George J. Coombes, 136–51, esp. 143–46, Winter makes similar claims for her rendition. Not all critics entirely agreed with Odell and Winter. The theater critic for the New York *Daily Tribune* wrote a very detailed commentary of her performance on 2 January 1882 at Booth's Theater, in which he criticized Anderson's Juliet for allowing her feelings to run away with her art. He also complained that she was too regal for the part. Nevertheless, he conceded that while she might not be perfect—and he was obviously hoping for an ideal Juliet—"she is the best our stage can boast." See Young, William C. 1975. *Famous Actors and Actresses of the American Stage.* 2 vols. New York: Bowker, 24–26.

16. Shakespeare's comedies seem to lend themselves to modern settings more easily than his tragedies or histories; see Berry, Ralph. 1989. *On Directing Shakespeare.* London: Hamish Hamilton, 14–16. If this is true, I am not sure why, although Berry suggests it may be because the stakes for fidelity to Shakespeare's original may be

higher. *Romeo and Juliet* violates this rule (if it is a rule), possibly because the first half is so comic. Not until Mercutio's death and Romeo's revenge against Tybalt does the play pivot around to tragedy.

17. Compare Worthen 1997, 141: "Putting Shakespeare on the modern stage may give us insight into our condition, but it doesn't change Shakespeare—it just dresses him in new clothes."

18. See Kennedy, Dennis. 1993. *Looking at Shakespeare.* Cambridge: Cambridge University Press, 297–300. Kennedy notes that at the end the prince spoke the first eight lines of the prologue instead of the familiar concluding lines of the play. He compares this curtailed ending with Henry Irving's a hundred years earlier. See also Clayton, Thomas. 1989. "'Balancing at Work': (R)evoking the Script in Performance and Criticism." *Shakespeare and the Sense of Performance*, edited by Marvin and Ruth Thompson. Newark: University of Delaware Press, 228–49. Clayton argues that "This *Romeo and Juliet* was a certain though unacknowledged adaptation, with the script seemingly as heavily ideologized with supertext as is easily possible without rewriting the script" (232). In more general terms, Clayton raises questions regarding the producer's and performers' responsibilities to the playwright, the script, the audience(s), "the best interests of society," etc., and distinguishes between an "exploitation production" and an "alienation production" (234 ff.).

19. Printed editions of the plays are another matter. Eighteenth-century acting editions often included passages cut in performance but market them with quotation marks or inverted commas.

20. The production was staged at the Khan Theater in Jerusalem in conjunction with a Palestinian group from Ram'allah. The director for the Hebrew part (Capulets) was Eran Baniel; for the Palestinian part (Montagues), Fuad Awad. I am grateful to Professor Avram Oz of the University of Haifa for this information.

21. See "Putting a New Slant on 'Romeo and Juliet.'" 1999. *The Washington Post*, 24 January, C7.

22. Compare Wimsatt, William K. 1954. "The Concrete Universal." In *The Verbal Icon*. Lexington: University of Kentucky Press, 69–83; and Worthen 1997, 65: "Yet while modern dress potentially narrows the play's frame of reference, it also universalizes it: Shakespeare was really writing about *us* all along."

23. Worthen 1997, 61. Compare Clayton 1989, who says that producers and performers should ask, "What fresh, striking, yet congenial means can I use to help the script to speak for itself and to us, our condition, and the resources of *our* theater (whatever it might be) at one and the same time."

"I Have done the deed": *Macbeth* 2.2

James P. Lusardi and June Schlueter

In a variety of ways but relentlessly, the authors in this collection will be making the same basic point: words on a page do not make a play. We want to make the point also, in our own way.

We begin by offering the example of Laurence Olivier as Macbeth in a moment from the 1955 Stratford-upon-Avon production of the play. The moment comes at 3.1.75 where Macbeth is greeting the two murderers he will suborn to kill Banquo. The words that the playtext gives Macbeth are "Well then, now . . . ,"[1] words apparently functioning just to complete a pentameter line, roughly equivalent to the "ah—ah—ah" speakers will resort to while collecting their thoughts. And, of course, the words can be played that way. Some Macbeths have used "Well then, now" as an opportunity to clear their throats. Not Olivier. Facing the murderers center stage, his gown a vivid red and his crown slightly atilt, he "eyed them mockingly." Then, he raised both hands and pointed at each murderer, putting "Well" as a question—"Well?" Pausing, he crooked each index finger to invite them to come closer, with a peremptory "then." When the murderers hesitated, he dropped his hands to point to the floor on either side of him and turned the final word into a "frightening imperative"—"Now!"[2]

We tell this story not because we wish to celebrate a much-celebrated actor but because we want to make it nakedly obvious that a playtext represents only a beginning for the performers of that text. Nor is it simply a matter of the actor being free to interpret the playtext. The actor acts under necessity: he or she is compelled to interpret the material provided by the playwright. To put it another way, the actor is necessarily, for good or ill, a creator of the performed play as surely as the playwright is. And the same may be said of the other collaborators in the production process: the director, the designers of various kinds, and the artisans who realize their designs. All are makers, whose product is a theatrical event. Or perhaps we should say theatrical experience. For the audience also participates in the process as an interpretive community whose responses, anticipated or actual, shape what is done with the playtext.

As anyone's attempt to read a playtext should show, it is hardly transparent in its generation of actions or the meanings of the actions. It is, rather, fraught with puzzles and ambiguities. In seeking to cope with the text and the story that it is telling us, we invariably, consciously or unconsciously, seek to discover the subtext, the story that informs that story. Take the play that is our subject. What is motivating or driving Macbeth to do what he does? Ambition? The weird sisters? His wife? These are three possible answers, routine answers as it happens, but even these three routine alternatives point up the ambiguity. If we go to Macbeth himself, we do not get much help. Macbeth is a character who thinks and feels in images, and these images, however powerful, are not fully articulate, especially when couched, as they often are, in syntactical convolutions. Macbeth is evidently both fascinated and horrified by what is happening to him, but he does not seem to understand it. And so the burden on his interpreters of figuring him out is a heavy one. But the actor taking the role must try to figure him out. In practical performance terms, this means that in the past and in our own time the role has been variously interpreted. To study or experience the play in production is to meet not one Macbeth but many, Olivier's being only one of the more notable. And although Lady Macbeth may seem to be less complex as a character, this role has proven to be just as elusive and challenging to its interpreters.

By way of focusing interpretive issues, we shall concentrate on *Macbeth* 2.2, the murder scene. We call it the "murder scene"—indeed, it is among the most famous murder scenes in all drama—and yet, remarkably, it omits the actual murder. Why does Shakespeare sacrifice this opportunity to present a compelling spectacle? What does this surprising omission tell us about the play he wrote? What gets his attention, and hence ours, instead? To put the matter simply, it is not the brutal murder of King Duncan but the reactions to it, supremely those of his protagonists, that capture his interest and command ours. It is not the bloody deed but the bloody thoughts, not the outward act but the inner life, that he invites us to scrutinize. This takes us right back to the questions we were just considering about what drives Macbeth and, by implication, Lady Macbeth to do what they do—and to the subtext that will inform the performance of the playtext.

How should or may the words of this climactic episode be performed—how realized in flesh and blood and action upon the stage?

To say that the exchange between Macbeth and Lady Macbeth in this scene is "climactic" is to acknowledge that it occurs in the context of other exchanges, those of the letter scene (1.5) and the persuasion scene (1.7). It also occurs in the context of each character's earliest self-reflexive monologues and meditations, Lady Macbeth's in 1.5 and Macbeth's in 1.3, 1.4, 1.7, and 2.1. In each case, the director and the actors will have made interpretive choices that color the approach to this scene, and, of course, the choices made here will affect the performance of scenes to come. Historically, in the staging of *Macbeth*, these choices have sometimes been dictated by long-standing theatrical tradition and a generally received conception of the two characters.

For example, in the eighteenth and early nineteenth centuries Lady Macbeth was what Marvin Rosenberg would call the "power" character. She drove and dominated her fretfully moral and vacillating husband. Such a fierce and formidable presence was Hannah Pritchard to David Garrick's Macbeth and Sarah Siddons to John Philip Kemble's. Pritchard is remembered in the murder scene as coolly in control, almost smiling, and Siddons as returning from Duncan's chamber wearing "the ghastly horrid smile of a 'triumphant fiend.' " Audiences at the time assumed that this interpretation of the characters was inevitable, that it was the only true way to perform this play. For a while, Siddons considered moderating her portrayal to make Lady Macbeth "fair, feminine, nay, even fragile," at least in appearance if not in spirit, but, finally, she didn't dare. Neither audiences nor critics would stand for it. Still, there were some advocates of a "softer" Lady Macbeth, a conception that gradually and, in a changing cultural context, inexorably gained ground, so that by the end of the nineteenth century Ellen Terry—startlingly blonde—was playing a wifely, affectionate, gently but firmly manipulative Lady Macbeth to Henry Irving's spectacularly villainous Macbeth.[3]

As even this sketch of stage history will suggest, interpretive choices are never innocent of the historical and cultural circumstances in which they are made. And we could easily add to the list of contingencies that shape the interpretation of any given production. Perhaps the best way to think of performance is that it is always an experimental process, a testing of the playtext to see what discoveries it will yield when the elements of the theatrical experience are in force.

In this experimental spirit and as a way of suggesting a range of interpretations, we have sometimes asked our students to improvise a performance of the first thirty-three lines of the murder scene, through Lady Macbeth's "so, it will make us mad." Rather than outline the entire exercise, we shall simply say that we use five couples and, taking each couple aside, ask them to prepare and perform the sequence according to different directions.[4] The separate directions we give to the couples are as follows:

(1) Lady Macbeth is domineering and ruthless and Macbeth, after doing the deed, remorseful and irresolute. (Essentially, the eighteenth-century reading.)
(2) Lady Macbeth is drunk; Macbeth is disgusted with her and with himself.
(3) Lady Macbeth is practical, businesslike; Macbeth is hysterical.
(4) Lady Macbeth and Macbeth are both terrorized by the event but are struggling to be mutually supportive.
(5) Lady Macbeth and Macbeth are a loving couple, at once disturbed and erotically excited by the murder.

While the directions are scarcely exhaustive, they do prove suggestive. As we've already noticed, every production of *Macbeth* and every exchange between husband and wife will establish a power dynamic between them, with each adopting a status higher or lower than that of the other. By design, our directions keep shifting the high-status/low-status relationship of the characters. In the first three vignettes, Lady Macbeth is alternately high, low, high, and Macbeth is the opposite; in the last two, the relationships are much closer, though in each case differently motivated, with power shifting back and forth between the two. Again, though the directions may seem somewhat extravagant, there are textual grounds for every one of them. Take number 2, for example. Lady Macbeth opens the scene with the lines "That which hath made them drunk hath made me bold; / What hath quenched them hath given me fire." If this utterance is not an admission of drunkenness, it is certainly an admission of drinking, perhaps heavy drinking. And if it is taken as a cue for performance, an implied stage direction, some interesting things begin to happen. Thus, Macbeth's "This is a sorry sight" (20) is usually interpreted in production according to a modern editor's interpolated stage directions: *Looking on his hands.*[5] While plausible, the interpretation is not inevitable, a point this improvisation has several times brought out. A disgusted Macbeth may find his "sorry sight" in Lady Macbeth, only later contemplating his "hangman's hands" when he says he does in line 27. And Lady Macbeth's "A foolish thought, to say a sorry sight" (21) may be purely defensive. Whether any of these specific readings is adopted, such testing of the playtext, if it forces us to see things freshly, does us a valuable service.

The murder scene is quintessential *Macbeth*. Though it is only seventy-three lines of text, all the central concerns of the play are here, and the special problems for its producers are neatly exemplified. We shall discuss both.

The scene shares the motifs of the larger play. It begins and ends with noises offstage. Moments before, at the end of 2.1, the ringing of a bell has summoned Macbeth to Duncan's chamber, and now Lady Macbeth startles at the owl's shriek, which she associates with the "fatal bellman['s]" message of death (3–4). The scene ends, of course, with the dreadful and repeated knocking at the gate (56, 64, 68, 72). Meantime, there are references to other noises and voices, both actual and imagined—shouts and cries, laughter and prayer, and the terrible refrain "Sleep no more . . . Macbeth shall sleep no more" (40–42). In fact, sleeping and waking represent another motif, from the "snores" of the grooms (6) at the beginning to Macbeth's "Wake Duncan with thy knocking" (73) at the end. Another verbal string features deeds and doing, for example, "th'attempt and not the deed / Confounds us" (10–11), "Had he not resembled / My father as he slept, I had done't" (12–13), "I have done the deed" (14), and so continuing through "To know my deed, 'twere best not know myself" (72). Finally, there are images that are both verbal and visual: daggers, hands, blood.

All of these motifs involve performance decisions. Thus, if stage directions leave no doubt about the knocking at the end of the scene, the shrieking of the owl and the crickets' cry (15) at the outset are only implied by the spoken word. Are these noises actually to be heard by an audience? More problematic is Macbeth's outcry at line 8—"Who's there? What, ho?"—since the treatment of this noise affects the very shaping of the scene. First, does Lady Macbeth hear it? Evidently, she does, because she herself exclaims "Alack!" (9), fearful that the deed is not done, and later she asks her husband "Did you not speak?" (16). Next, and this is the more critical question, where is Macbeth when he makes this outcry? Do his words come from *within*, that is, offstage, or are they spoken onstage?

Although almost all modern editions indicate that Macbeth's words come from *within*, the 1623 Folio text, the only early text of the play, specifies that Macbeth makes his entrance with the line "Who's there? What, ho?",[6] not at line 13 where it is usually placed, presumed to be signaled by Lady Macbeth's greeting "My husband!" Why do modern editors almost invariably alter the Folio text, and why do modern producers of the play almost invariably accept this alteration? Well, as Alan Dessen points out, the "logic of verisimilitude" dictates it: "How are we to imagine a Macbeth onstage but not noticed by his wife for five lines?"[7] Notably, two editions that preserve the Folio entrance, R. A. Foakes's edition (1968) and the Norton edition (1997), suggest ways of accommodating it. Norton has Macbeth enter *above* to speak his line, then exit immediately, and then reenter *below* at line 13.[8] This solution is having it both ways, but, since Macbeth speaks of "descend[ing]" in line 16, it is plausible and actable. Foakes boldly stays with the Folio: "It is likely," he observes, that Macbeth "is on-stage, exhausted and bloody, seen by the audience but not at once by his wife, and slowly coming toward her."[9]

This reading is, in fact, close to Dessen's proposed staging when he tries to "imagine the scene as scripted in the Folio."[10] But Dessen has an additional interpretive point to make. He links the failure of Lady Macbeth to see her husband—"not-seeing"—in the play and specifically in the murder scene with her failure to notice the bloody daggers in Macbeth's bloody hands, another interpretive crux that we shall soon address.[11]

Certainly, Lady Macbeth's opening lines show her to be absorbed by thoughts of the murder in progress, at once confident and anxious about its consummation. But what are we to make of her reflection "Had he not resembled / My father as he slept, I had done't" (12–13)? It's apparently an expression of filial piety that implicates Duncan, but, if so, it indicates that she retains emotions she claims to repudiate in 1.5: "Make thick my blood; / Stop up th' access and passage of remorse, / That no compunctious visitings of nature / Shake my fell purpose" (41–44). It may, therefore, be taken as a sign of vulnerability. But much will depend on the actor's nuanced reading of the line. If the emphasis falls not on the opening clause but on the main clause—"I had done't"—the effect will be different, asserting instead the ferocity necessary to commit the murder. This effect, moreover, will be enhanced if she addresses the line not just to herself but directly to the audience. Another question involves Macbeth. Does he overhear the line? If he is indeed onstage when she speaks, he may not only hear it but seems to cap it with "*I* have done the deed" (14)—here we supply emphasis appropriate to such an interpretation. But what does he make of her line? For instance, does it contribute to his own agony of remorse because Duncan was like a father to him?

At this point, even before Macbeth makes his announcement, and whether or not he makes his entrance here, Lady Macbeth is suddenly aware of his presence. Her response is notable: "My husband." This is the first and only time in the play that she calls Macbeth husband. How does she do it? In the Folio text, the phrase is isolated as a single line, as if figuratively to italicize it, and it is punctuated with a question mark. Is it then a startled question? Almost all modern editors punctuate it with an exclamation point, as they have a warrant to do, since the Folio compositors make question marks do double duty as exclamation points. The line then becomes, perhaps, a thrilling assertion of partnership. But the possible shadings are many. Whether Lady Macbeth's reaction is startled or jubilant or something else, is there touching between them when they meet—a bloody handclasp, an embrace, a kiss? In performance, choices must be made.

The staccato dialogue between them entails a rather disjunctive series of questions, answers, and observations. At first, they seem to be talking about practical matters: "Didst thou not hear a noise?" (14); "Did you not speak?" (16). But Macbeth is not thinking about the same kind of noise that Lady Macbeth is, as soon becomes clear. And he suddenly breaks off in inquiry about the sleeping arrangements of the Duncan party to observe "This is a sorry sight" (20), a short line in both modern editions and in the Folio, implying an emphatic pause. As already mentioned, though it is undefined in the text, the pronoun "This" is conventionally and plausibly taken to refer to his bloody hands, especially because Macbeth explicitly refers to his "hangman's hands" seven lines later. But if Macbeth twice calls attention to his own bloody condition at this point, why does it take Lady Macbeth another twenty-odd lines to notice the daggers? Of course, in productions concerned with the "logic of verisimilitude," the weapons may be variously concealed—tucked in his belt, covered by a garment, held in one hand out of Lady Macbeth's sight while he extends his other hand. Yet the audience has to be acutely aware of the daggers; as Foakes remarks, the vision of the blade smeared with "gouts of blood" in the soliloquy at the end of 2.1 "here is made actual on the stage."[12] It may well be, as Dessen urges, that the daggers are visible to the playgoer but not seen by Lady Macbeth, and that the playgoer witnesses "not one but two striking examples of 'not-seeing' in the Folio version of the scene." He asks, "is not an audience better prepared for the sleep-walking (and her seeing or imagining there) or for the banquet scene when no one but Macbeth sees the ghost?"[13]

In the present context, Lady Macbeth is dismissive of the "sorry sight" and, in any case, eager to get away from the crime scene. But Macbeth will not respond to her urgency. Just as he was earlier in the play, he is "rapt" by his own thoughts, remembering the "noise" he heard or hallucinated in the corridor outside Duncan's chamber:

> There's one did laugh in's sleep, and one cried "Murder!"
> That they did wake each other. I stood and heard them.
> But they did say their prayers and addressed them
> Again to sleep.
>
> (22–25)

Although Lady Macbeth tries to be practical, she is riveted by her husband's reliving or reimagining of the moments after the murder, by his distress because "'Amen' / Stuck in my throat" (31–32), by his agonized arias on sleep and the "voice" that cried "Macbeth shall sleep no more" (42). As Rosenberg notes, she realizes that the danger is "not from without now, but from within Macbeth—and perhaps within her, too"[14]: "Consider it not so deeply" (29); "it will make us mad" (33); "What do you mean?" (39); "Who was it that thus cried?" (43).

Now that staccato dialogue has given way to despairing meditation, how are Macbeth's obsessive lyricism and Lady Macbeth's anxious rejoinders to be expressed onstage? Does Macbeth show resentment toward his wife for his suffering, or does he invite her to share in it? Is Lady Macbeth's alarm at his behavior laced with contempt or sympathy? What do they do on the stage? Do they remain still or move about? Does Macbeth fall on his knees in the throes of his despair? Does Lady Macbeth listen to him fixedly or try to stop her ears? Does she shush him, perhaps even put her hand over his mouth? If she does, does he react angrily or submissively? All of these things and many more have been played in the scene.

The baffled Lady Macbeth may be severe or comforting or uneasy as she reminds Macbeth of the "noble strength" (44) he is neglecting and as she prompts him to "wash this filthy witness from your hand" (46). Since she refers to only one hand, she may have seen only one and hence failed to notice the daggers in the other. But if she has seen both hands brandishing the daggers, it is only here that she actually registers their presence.

This is a key moment in the play and in the scene. Macbeth has borne the "badges of his crime" from the place of the crime:[15] he cannot and will not be able to separate himself from it. Lady Macbeth must wash her own hands in Duncan's blood, and her doing so will be stamped indelibly on her psyche: she will remember and reenact this moment and its bloody sequel later when sleepwalking (5.1). Now, horrified at the lapse of her husband, she orders him to return the daggers and to "smear / The sleepy grooms with blood" (48–49). He won't do it, can't do it, and so she must do it. Her "Infirm of purpose!" may be thundered or whispered or wept. Again, no stage direction accompanies her command "Give me the daggers" (52) to mark the point of transfer. The exchange can occur at various points during this speech that ends with her exit at line 56. In a fury, she may at once seize the daggers from Macbeth's hands. Or she may struggle with her husband, prying each dagger from his clutching fingers as she speaks. Or she may wait, still trying to shame him into the task while the daggers rattle with his trembling, only at length snatching them from him. Her grim pun about "gild[ing]" the faces of the grooms to show "their guilt" (55–56) has been spoken to herself as an effort of the will or shared with Macbeth as a bright idea.

At her exit, the knocking at the gate begins. Should it be soft or loud? Most productions make it loud, and it gets progressively louder. The outside world is impinging on a scene of domestic horror. Macbeth doesn't know where the noise is coming from—"Whence is that knocking?" (56). He only knows that it appalls him. But there is something that he finds more appalling: "What hands are here?" His fix on his bloody hands, like his earlier fix on sleep, generates another lyrical expression of the enormity of his crime:

> Will all great Neptune's ocean wash this blood
> Clean from my hand? No, this hand will rather
> The multitudinous seas incarnadine,
> Making the green one red.
>
> (59–62)

While Macbeth's passion issues in this richly suggestive mix of resonant polysyllables and stark monosyllables, what is he doing? Many Macbeths simply stare fixedly at their hands. Others have rubbed or tried to wipe them or even struck the offending hands against each other. Still others have stretched out their arms in an effort to repudiate their own hands. But most Macbeths bring their hands close to their faces. Ian McKellen virtually clawed at his face on "they pluck out mine eyes" (58), then scrutinized his hands only inches away, and finally extended his arms and waved them rhythmically. Occasionally, Macbeths have literally washed their hands in an onstage bucket or well. Far better was the "despairing, fumbling abhorrence with which Olivier sought to ward off the multitudinous seas of blood that seemed to be swirling about his very knees."[16]

Lady Macbeth's return, which parallels Macbeth's entrance at the beginning of the scene, may be gradual or sudden and surprising to her husband. She expresses the same concern—"My hands are of your color"—but in sensibility she belongs to a different order of being: "I shame / To wear a heart so white . . . A little water clears us of this deed" (63–64, 66). So it may seem to her. She apparently thinks the murder of Duncan will finish the business. Those who know the play know better: there is no end to the murder. They also know that Lady Macbeth will engage in an agonizing reenactment of this sequence in her sleepwalking scene (5.1). The actor in the part of Lady Macbeth, therefore, has some options here. She may be glib and practical in her managing of affairs as her lines suggest she is: "Retire we to our chamber" (65); "Get on your nightgown" (69). Or she may, in various ways, signal a distress that belies her words. She may return breathless and trembling. She may involuntarily retch in disgust at her gory hands. She may consciously or unconsciously rub and wipe her hands, anticipating her actions in 5.1. Or her bravado may strike a false note, seeming rehearsed for the occasion. Whatever her mode of denial, sincere or suspect, there is for her no denying of the condition in which she finds her husband.

Macbeth may be raving when she returns, but usually he is staggered and even paralyzed by his reflections. He is certainly speechless, until the very end of the scene, while Lady Macbeth seeks alternately to reprove, reassure, and direct him. He may be startled at her reentry and intermittently attentive to her words and to the knocking. Or he may be almost totally absorbed by his bloody hands and lost in his thoughts, "poorly" (71) as his wife would have it. Macbeth knows that his deed has defined him: "To know my deed, 'twere best not know myself" (72). As the knocking becomes more insistent, the urgency of their departure intensifies. But about the manner of it the text is silent: the sole stage direction is an unrevealing *Exeunt*. Fortunately, the sleepwalking scene may be taken to provide a gloss on their exit. As she relives the moment in her trance-like state, Lady Macbeth gives direction: "To bed, to bed! There's knocking at the gate. Come, come, come, come, give me your hand!" (5.1.61–62). As she has earlier in the scene, she must again try to control her husband. This proves to be difficult. Some Macbeths finally succumb to her appeals and follow her or accompany her off, their partnership now sealed in blood. But others, stunned and stupefied, seem impervious to her pleadings. They need to be physically taken from the stage. Sometimes a handclasp will do it. Often it requires Lady Macbeth's frantic tugging and pulling or pushing as Macbeth shouts for the waking of Duncan. And bloody hands complicate the effort. Gasping and grunting, Jane Lapotaire desperately pushes against her husband's back with the heels of her hands. Judi Dench, extending both arms to keep her hands clear, catches her mesmerized Macbeth in a grotesque embrace, the crook of her elbow at his neck, and walks him off backwards, as he quietly retches out the line "Wake Duncan with thy knocking! I would thou couldst" (73).

As much as we have said about 2.2 in text and in performance, there is much we have ignored. For example, we have pointedly said nothing about costuming and set design or stage furniture. Partly, this is because of time limitations, but it is also because of the nature of the scene, with its tight focus on the intense interaction of two characters. Apart from a set that may be on two levels, with stairs providing access to the above, the scene requires little except for hand properties and stage blood. And though costumes would contribute to the texture of the scene in production, we have seen it powerfully performed in street clothes. Had our subject been the banquet scene (3.4) or the apparition scene (4.1), our strategy would have been different. Still, to make up for our omissions and, more important, to show the scene as it has in fact been realized, we shall conclude with samplings of four productions that vary in genre and in approach. All are on tape.[17]

(1) The first is a 1981 production, with Philip Anglim and Maureen Anderman, directed by Sarah Caldwell at Lincoln Center. The video version is simply a tape of a live performance with a full audience in attendance. Rather operatic in style and period staging, with a great deal of movement above and below, the murder scene presents a Lady Macbeth who dominates her cringing husband.

(2) Roman Polanski's well-known 1971 *Macbeth* has no links with the stage. It is a "film film," as our students like to say, and it fully exploits filmic conventions in a version scripted by Kenneth Tynan and Polanski that seeks to recreate a medieval world. Unlike Shakespeare's play, the film features the brutal murder of Duncan as well as its aftermath. In a somewhat abbreviated treatment of 2.2, a young Francesca Annis plays a childish and whimpering wife to Jon Finch's stony-faced Macbeth.

(3) Jack Gold's 1982 *Macbeth* was made for the BBC-TV series, "The Shakespeare Plays." Though it has no direct connections with the stage, Nicol Williamson and Jane Lapotaire are seasoned veterans of the theater. Williamson had previously played Macbeth for the RSC in 1974–75 opposite Helen Mirren, and Lapotaire appeared in the same production as one of the witches and Lady Macduff. In Gold's version of the murder scene, the relationship between the principles is more complex than in the Caldwell and Polanski versions and, we think, more interesting. In a stylized world of castles, Williamson's Macbeth is a man of action who towers over the loving Lapotaire; and yet the murder scene reduces him to a hysteria from which she must desperately seek to recover him.

(4) In 1976, Trevor Nunn mounted a production for the RSC at The Other Place in Stratford-upon-Avon. It starred Judi Dench and Ian McKellen. It was virtually a studio production, highly stylized and ritualized, with actors seated in a circle around the playing space in quasi-modern dress. The props were simple and relatively few, chief among them a golden robe and crown, and the lighting effects, often chiaroscuro, were stunning. The production ran for three years, moving to the Stratford mainstream and then to the Warehouse and the Young Vic in London. It was remade for TV in 1978. In the murder scene, Dench exhibits extraordinary variety as she interacts with an equally compelling McKellen as he succumbs to overmastering self-absorption.

Notes

1. Citations of *Macbeth* are to Harbage, Alfred, ed. 1969. *The Complete Pelican Shakespeare*. Revised edition. Baltimore: Penguin, 1110–35.

2. See Evans, Gareth Lloyd. 1982. "*Macbeth*: 1946–80 at Stratford-upon-Avon." In *Focus on "Macbeth,"* edited by John Russell Brown. London: Routledge and Kegan Paul, 99. And Rosenberg, Marvin. 1978. *The Masks of Macbeth*. Berkeley: University of California Press, 400–401. The accounts of Olivier's actions vary slightly.

3. All citations in this paragraph are to Rosenberg, Marvin. 1982. "Macbeth and Lady Macbeth in the eighteenth and nineteenth centuries." In Brown, *Focus on "Macbeth,"* 74, 77, 84–85. See also Rosenberg 1978, 67–72, 92–94; and Kliman, Bernice E. 1992. *Shakespeare in Performance: Macbeth.* Manchester: Manchester University Press, 24–39.

4. For accounts of this exercise and others, see Lusardi, James P. 1992. "Shakespeare's Performed Words: *Macbeth* and Improvisation in the Classroom." *CEA Critic* 54.2 (Winter): 23–28.

5. See *Macbeth*, for example, in Evans, G. Blakemore, ed. 1997. *The Riverside Shakespeare.* Boston: Houghton Mifflin, 2.2.17 sd. And in Greenblatt, Stephen, Cohen, Walter, Howard, Jean and Maas, K. E., ed. 1997. *The Norton Shakespeare.* New York: W.W. Norton, 2.2.18 sd.

6. Hinman, Charlton, ed. 1968. *The First Folio of Shakespeare.* New York: W.W. Norton, 744.

7. Dessen, Alan C. 1995. *Recovering Shakespeare's Theatrical Vocabulary.* Cambridge: Cambridge University Press, 103.

8. *Macbeth* in Greenblatt et al. 1997, 2.2.8–13 and sds.

9. Foakes, R. A., ed. 1968. *Macbeth.* New York: Bobbs-Merrill, 2.2.8 sd and note.

10. Dessen 1995, 104.

11 Ibid.

12. Foakes, R. A. "Images of Death: Ambition in *Macbeth.*" In Brown, *Focus on "Macbeth,"* 17.

13. Dessen 1995, 104–5.

14. Rosenberg 1978, 334.

15. Ibid., 339.

16. Ibid., 344–45.

17. For information on the Polanski film and the BBC and RSC videos, see Rothwell, Kenneth S., and Annabelle Henken Melzer. 1990. *Shakespeare on Screen: An International Filmography and Videography.* New York: Neal-Schuman, nos. 324, 336, 332. The video of the Caldwell Lincoln Center production, which seems to have escaped Rothwell and Melzer's net, is distributed by Films for the Humanities, PO Box 2053, Princeton, NJ 08543–2053.

Disguise in Trevor Nunn's *Twelfth Night*

H. R. Coursen

Disguise is used in different ways in *As You Like It* and *Twelfth Night*. Rosalind may cry "Alas the day! What shall I do with my doublet and hose?" but she uses her disguise to develop a mode of courtship that gets a number of issues out of the way before heterosexuality rears its head—and, it follows, before she marries Orlando. For Viola, disguise is a knot that only time and an identical twin can untie.

Neither of these scripts has translated well to film or TV. Identical twins don't play in naturalistic media where our willing suspension of disbelief is not part of the implicit contract between audience and production. A film like *Shakespeare in Love* insists that we *believe* in the convention of the boy actor on the Elizabethan stage. Master Kent may play the *male* lead, but we are rooting for her to succeed in defying the restriction against women on the Elizabethan stage. Her transgression of both gender role and stage convention is meant to serve a normalization of gender on stage. For one glorious afternoon, she succeeds. She gets to play Juliet in Will's new play. The film trades on the frantic untrussing of the boy actor backstage and on the boy actor naked in bed and objecting because Will is stealing "her" lines as Romeo. The lad, whose voice has yet to change (and never will), possesses elements of female physicality that finally become apparent to the world (the Globe), though hidden for the time being for the sake of the fiction that both film and play within the film depict. This Juliet is forced into her stereotypic role at the end. She must marry Paris, here known as Wessex.

The disguising of gender in Shakespeare becomes an intersection at which the issue of sexuality can be explored. The interrogation involves an artistic neutrality—that negative capability of which Keats speaks—within which actors deal with a gendered subtext. A woman in drag, says Holly Burbach, "will undermine the ideology of masculinity" (1999). That is true, whether the subtext is the "hidden woman's fear" that the tentative Rosalind knows will lurk beneath her disguise, or the posturing of the "fine, bragging youth" that the more confident Portia will imitate. The disguises involve a bringing forward of energy—even stereotypic assumptions—at the service of the change in gender. This is not the radical readjustment of Brecht's Shui Ta, from a kindly woman to a brutal man, the exchange of one stereotype for the other. In Shakespeare, two identities uncover a third in a zone where psychic integration can occur. Disguise opens an area within which the character can explore the dimensions, physical and psychological, of a role, instead of merely playing the surfaces and expectations of an external mask. Shakespeare gives the actor plenty of scope here, insisting that she bring her own experience, as actor and as person, to the process. The scripts are written to insist on a remarkable interplay of character, role assumed, and actor. Orlando or Orsino does not merely get to know a Ganymede or Cesario before the opposite gender presents itself, but to transform his own stereotypic assumptions about gender into something far more deeply interfused. That something has resonated out from the impersonation that Rosalind and Viola have created. An undermining of the ideology of masculinity provides a mirror for the undermining of the postures of Orlando and Orsino. If a production convinces us of this complex but comic process, we can believe the happy ending and take it with us.

In the 1996 RSC *Twelfth Night*, Clive Wood's Orsino kissed Emma Fielding's Cesario as he/she left for another embassy to Olivia. Orsino backed away, touching his mouth. Who am I? It was an interrogation of his own arrogance, a step toward a recognition of his love for the person in the male garments. For the first time, the nobleman was experiencing what F. D. Laing calls "ontological uncertainty." "Shakespeare in Love" borrows that moment at the end of the taxi ride from Bankside to Lady Viola's wharf. It is a forbidden attraction (of Will to the "boy") that reinforces another forbidden attraction (of Will to a woman who is out of his welkin). One of the joys of the film is its movement back and forth from gender role to gender role, using the boy actor as the central pivot around which the issue of gender is engaged. The lines of *Romeo and Juliet* become exchangeable, interchangeable, roaming from bed to stage, from boy actor who is a girl playing Romeo, to boy actor who is a boy playing Juliet, becoming at moments a duet between the playwright and his male lead, transformed into Botticelli's Venus once she has let her hair down.

For Viola, it is a question of how do I get out of this role? For Dustin Hoffman's Tootsie, the disguised man wants to be a man right out.

Brother and sister are not identical twins, but are identical. Tootsie's doffing of her disguise is meant to show his beloved (Jessica Lange) that Tootsie is a he and therefore ready for a heterosexual beginning. Courtship by disguise is over. Jessica, though, has just watched her friend, her confidant, her surrogate mother—someone she wants to *stay* that way—remove eyelashes and wig, and has heard the voice of her most hated enemy—a man. They reconcile, however, as Hoffman says, "I was a better man with you as a woman than I ever was with a woman as a man . . . I've got to learn to do it without a dress. The hard part's over. We were already good friends." He has accepted the female in himself, well and good, but can Jessica accept the male? The film implies that the issue is not crucial. It is the man, it seems, the Orlando or Orsino, who must surrender his early posturing for an identity that can include another person within both its psychic and social structures. In *Tootsie* we do not witness, as we do in *As You Like It* and *Twelfth Night*, the woman's role in educating the man. The reason, of course, is that it is the man who is disguised. It may seem sexist to insist that it is the *male* education that is at issue, but the implication is that the woman is already psychologically in command of her identity. She is, for example, too knowing to try to play a man "straight." She is already aware of the unconscious quality beneath the actions and attitudes of the stereotypic male.

Nunn's brilliant film shows Olivia's need to escape her role of mourning. Feste pulls her veil back, and the camera circles, demonstrating Olivia's ranging sexuality. Later, Cesario shouts "Olivia!" The bracken trembles. Malvolio spins around, his hairpiece ruffled. Even the crows pick up the echo. In a Shakespeare & Company production of 1992, Tom Jaeger doubled as Malvolio and Sebastian. The transition from Malvolio's dark house to Sebastian's glorious sun was made by the same actor, one character stepping into the fantasies of another. Sebastian was what lay under Malvolio. The latter had read Olivia aright and had been encouraged to translate her sexual resonance in his direction. The film shows Olivia in a disguise she is eager to doff, thus fulfilling Gloria Steinem's bitter dictum that "Women have been female impersonators for a long time" (Kimmel, 1999).

The film occurs in early autumn, the time of Keats's "mist and mellow fruitfulness." Mist washes the empty choirs of the oak, and apples await their baskets in Olivia's orchards. It is not a cherry orchard, we notice. Olivia's destructive sexuality will be socially absorbed, unlike Lyuba's. Orsino's castle rests on an island, along a causeway open only at low tide. It is a dream castle, often viewed from a distance, an outcropping of consciousness scarcely rising above the surface. There, Orsino reclines while his officers stand and wait for orders. His right arm is in a sling, a synecdoche for inactivity, perhaps as a result of a wound received in the battle of which Antonio speaks. This Orsino is a version of Meredith's Willoughby Patterne in *The Egoist*. The film, for Stephen Holden, is a "moody, pre-Freudian allegory" (1996, C3). John Mullan says that "darkness prevails over the early scenes. . . . a velvet gloom. . . . This is to be a somber comedy" (20). Olivia lives, though, above a vast kitchen over which Malvolio presides, duke of the downstairs. Appetite is underneath. Upstairs, the curtains are drawn against the watery autumn light, but the rich hangings, painted Italian wallpaper, and deep Persian rugs suggest, as Anthony Lane says "A sumptuous relish in [Olivia's] mourning" (74). A painting of her manor house hangs in the living room, meaning that Olivia does not have to go outside to see the outside. Hers is a Thackerayan world in which the widow's weeds must be carefully cut, the roast for the mourners done rarely, the port so fine that the connoisseur will remark upon it, and beg a bottle after the funeral, where Jos's dying father precludes his son from giving "any *large* parties this year." Between castle and manor house, a fishing village is patrolled by Orsino's ominous mounted police. At one point, while they are chasing Antonio, the soldiers upset a cart and slither around a corner on a carpet of seaweed and hake. The image links the primal energy of the sea with the festive tables of the rich. The piano at which Sebastian and Viola had played their game aboard the ship becomes a tinkling set of keys washed to silence on the shore. They are replaced by the pianos and songs of Illyria, a peninsula full of harmonies waiting to be heard.

In the film's first scene, in the doomed ship's salon, Sebastian and Viola disguise as oriental princesses, veiled from the nose down. *He* is in the reverse gender role. He removes her moustache. She seems about to remove his—is it also false?—when the ship discerns its rock. The moustache lends a false maturity to Sebastian—though later it does seem to be home grown—and a false gender to Viola, when she redisguises herself on the beach. The moustaches link up with Malvolio's toupee, an effort at reversing time, as opposed to advancing it. Olivia is veiled and hiding an aspect of her maturing gender—her sexuality—when the mustachioed Viola enters the dark room and whispers for "the lady of the house." Little things add up here and remind us that we are witnessing linked moments of a single event. The treatment of Sebastian and Viola builds, it would seem, on Thomas Bouchard's classic study of identical twins, reinforced recently by William Wright (1998). The identity games these twins play reinforce the psychological masquerade performed by so many of the inhabitants of Illyria, as Feste keeps pointing out.

Viola's disguise becomes Nunn's metaphor within a naturalistic medium. The issues are, what is gender? what are gender stereotypes in the late nineteenth century of the film's mise-en-scène? what are the limits of stereotype? The film, for all of its fidelity to "Shakespeare," speaks directly to the late twentieth century. That is not the result of an "imposed vision." Shakespeare was asking the same questions. "Is it possible," Nunn asks, "that what is feminine in men is extraordinarily attractive to women, and what is male in [the] female is extraordinarily attractive to men?" (Marks 1996, H18). Nunn embraces wholeheartedly the convention of girl become boy within which a portion of this interrogation can be launched. It is important, says Nunn, that spectators not "get off the hook of the play by dismissing it as an improbable archaic comedy" (Fineline 1996, 4), that they recognize what they *share* with the characters. The "movie suggests that an essential sexual ambiguity exists in all of us," as Holden says, particularly "once the defining sexual plumage of one sex has been exchanged for that of another" (C3). Viola has already learned to don a moustache, so that her use of the clothes that survive in the salt stained trunk is not a sudden contrivance but an organic development of the charade.* Imogen Stubbs is a fine comic actor in the tradition of Harold Lloyd, and certainly the most nuanced Viola/Cesario I have seen since Eileen Atkins at the Old Vic in the late 1970s. The camera closes up on the smaller moments when Stubbs responds to the role she is playing and enforces our belief in her intrinsic character and gender—and in who she longs to be. It may be that the woman playing the man does *not* fall into the stereotypic wishes that the role incorporates—like Hoffman as Tootsie wishing "she" could be pretty, or the boy actor in *Shakespeare in Love* angry because his dress makes him "look like a

---

* The trunk discovered on the beach goes back to the first (and apparently only) silent *Twelfth Night*, Vitagraph's one-reel version of 1910, where, according to the initial caption, Viola "dresses herself from her brother's trunk, cast up by the sea" (Ball 1968, 56).

pig."* The corollary here is that Orsino takes Cesario at face value, an assessment that makes her outer role easier but that complicates things for the woman beneath the cadet's outfit, particularly since Orsino is very attracted to this boy. On stage, the effects are often exaggerated—Orsino's clap on the back, his masculine arm comradely around the lad's shoulder.

Stubbs's Cesario masters the male game. It is not easy. One has to smoke fell and cruel cigars, chafe from riding horses astride, and play snooker. She hits a great shot, kissing a ball into a corner pocket, surprising herself and snookering Orsino. The camera shows us both reactions—her amazement followed by an "Aw shucks!" shrug and, behind her, his incredulity. Stubbs teaches us to suspend our disbelief. Her performance, much of it for our eyes only, shows that the male role is built on a fragile structure of acquired skills resting on a foundation of arrogance. It needs the relaxation into a wider, less codified role that the *anima*—the female minority element in the male psyche—can achieve if not repressed. A large factor in the tragedy of Macbeth is that he already possesses the milk of human kindness. Lady Macbeth drives him toward the masculine stereotype, and soon, as opposed to having a "nature . . . full of the milk of human kindness," his "mind" is "full of scorpions." They exchange orientations as the play moves along. He becomes the unreflecting murderer (though something in him keeps reminding him of his humanity) and she becomes the terrified woman who cannot abide the smell of blood (even as everything in her reminds *us* of her humanity). Nunn's *Twelfth Night* shows Orsino's icy narcissism melt to warmth for Cesario. Viola personifies what Orsino must learn to be, what he must find in himself, that in him that Cesario loves in spite of his masculine posturing. The film shows the process at work. As Cesario finds the man, she finds the man. As she masters the male stereotype, her feminine qualities master Orsino. Their identities melt together finally at a level that permits us to enjoy the comedy within our own imaginations.

Crossdressing was, of course, a staple of the silent screen, as in Nielsen's Hamlet, and in Marion Davies, whose "triumph is in her

*Once Portia tries to prove her manly stoicism by wounding herself. Another hopes that those observing her in disguise will "think [she is] accomplished With that [she] lack[s]." Lady Macbeth wishes to be *un*sexed. Viola longs for a "beard . . . though [she] would not have it grow on [her] chin." Her aside is also a wry comment on the convention of boy actor.

ability to create accurately the physical sense of a male in her movements, gestures, and reactions . . . Her goal is comic androgyny, and she burlesques masculine behavior while maintaining physical credibility" (Basinger 1999, 328). Davies—like Stubbs with the cigar—"becomes ill after puffing on a pipe" (321). Stubbs, however, is not "burlesquing" masculine behavior. She is trying very hard to acquire it physically, with that amusing earnestness that, I think, is built into the character. We smile but sympathize. The effect of burlesque—or satire—is to draw attention to the object imitated, and to general tendencies, not sympathy toward the character. Stubbs shows how difficult masculine behavior *is* to acquire and maintain—it is based on physical conditioning and often on an aggressive use of the body—but that is a secondary effect of her performance.*

Nunn tells us why he did not have Stubbs play both Sebastian and Viola (as Joan Plowright had done in a late 1960s TV version): "the audience is not the object of the joke, it must be in on the joke" (Fineline 1996, 5). In attempting to make Shakespeare "relevant" by adjusting the surface conditions of production, a director renders the script irrelevant to any but a very limited moment in a given culture, just as the narrowest of multicultural curricula are irrelevant—we must read only about ourselves, our race, our gender, our sexual orientation. Our narcissism permits nothing but a reflection of ourselves. This play explores gender issues—crossdressing, androgyny, homoeroticism, and even that most scorned of marginal positions, heterosexuality. A good production of *Twelfth Night* will use the text to interrogate those issues and thus to question our own cultural assumptions, as opposed to showing how narrowly trendy the script can be made to be.

Other aspects of the film reinforce Nunn's emphasis on gender, its construction and misconstruction. Malvolio woos the naked but armless statue in the garden, just as Oliva is moving from her frozen role of still unravished bride of repression to hot pursuit of Cesario. What he imagines happening *is* happening, but not to him. He believes that Olivia is a Galatea given life by the Aphrodite hovering

---

*Garbo's great crossdressing role in *Queen Christina* is brief, requires only a slight deepening of her already husky voice, and awaits only her unmasking in the bedroom by John Gilbert, whose bedroom she had shared many years before, in that lifetime ago Hollywood of the silent screen. Dustin Hoffman's Tootsie is more convincing as a woman—to Jessica Lange, at least—than he is as his male character.

in Maria's letter and its post scripts. The fountain in front of the garden and the walls of its inner yard are made of seashells. Elements of a wild and unseen kingdom have been domesticated into designs without being understood as themselves, as nurturers of life that are not meant to be the mere decorations of human beings. The statue, for all of its erotic qualities, is a domesticated piece of marble crafted by a male eye and arm. It is like the Duke's painting in the Browning poem and like the Duke's next duchess, an "object," a projection, an image controlled by the male observer. The armless Venus in the pagan garden is an emblem of Malvolio's fantasies, a fusion of the ideal and the sensual, like Keats's urn. It cannot speak back, therefore establishes none of the troublesome field of energy in which human interchange occurs. It cannot fend off. It can only absorb, and, in its voluptuousness, encourage projection. The importation of a "romance ending" into the scene—this one specifically from *The Winter's Tale*—lends poignancy to Malvolio's daydreams. Leontes—for better or worse—was born a king. He can command Hermione's trial and, after sixteen years, become the beneficiary of his repentance. Olivia is coming alive, but she can never live for Malvolio. Nunn picks up visually the qualifications that Keir Elam provides: "Malvolio's deciphering of Olivia's false epistle posits her body as a set of graphic signifiers, and thus as a corpus, a text, but at the same time it puts us on guard about over hasty reading of the body text" (Elam 1996, 148). It is worth noting that Maria can dictate fantasies—perhaps having some of her own, as the film suggested during the carpe diem song in the kitchen.

Both Orsino and Olivia also "misread Viola's body text" until a second misreading—Olivia's of Sebastian—straightens things out. Viola, in disguise, is not for Olivia, nor is the concealed Olivia—neither body nor its desire—for Malvolio. The naked statue in the garden neatly links two of the play's plots by means of the misreading of bodies. This emphasis is made again at the end, when Orsino insists that Viola appear *as* woman before further ceremonies occur. While the film cuts the lines about Malvolio's controlling the trunk containing Viola's woman's weeds, they suggest that Malvolio must agree, however unwillingly, to the establishment of relations that the end of the play confirms, even if he himself is left out (in the rain) of the final festivities.

The film's Andrew looks like Cesario, a resemblance I found confusing at times. Cesario, though, is learning to do the things—even "against the mettle of her sex"—that Andrew has never learned. For the first time in any *Twelfth Night* that I have ever seen, Cesario defends herself against an Andrew who can't even be a vicarious bully. Cesario underlines the gender distinction for us by delivering a golata to Andrew's most vulnerable zone. Andrew is specifically the "Rudesby" whom Olivia dismisses. He has attempted, against all the odds, to seize the afternoon and approach her. He does achieve a certain dignity in his departure from Olivia in the final scene and perhaps gives us there a hint about how he might have been played earlier, so that he would have been a subject not just of slapstick but of pathos as well.

Shakespeare in Love suggests that gender matters, but its qualities are fulfilled when people in love can exchange roles and say each other's lines and express them with the singleness of their passion. One beauty of the film is that love itself is arrested at its height—just beyond the moment of Keats's lover on that urn. Viola will, for Will, forever be Miranda, even as he moves into crabbed old age with his Prospero.

A recent Subaru commercial shows a beautiful woman subduing the representative of an evil empire, and making her escape in what looks like a Subaru. Another car—was that a Honda?—fails to make it through the closing doors of the warehouse. The masculine does not feminize the feminine here. That's Crocodile Dundee under the rubber mask! The feminine has been the site whereon surprise is enacted. The revelation of a masculine subtext is, by 1999, unnecessary.

Storm, Fire, and Blood: Patterns of Imagery in Stuart Burge's *Julius Caesar*

Harry Keyishian

FOCUSING ON FILM RATHER THAN THEATER, THIS PAPER AIMS TO EXPAND the concept of Shakespearean performance criticism to include the distinctive contribution made by the art of cinematography. It also suggests ways that film can be used in the classroom to alert students to the possibilities of language and the ways patterns of verbal imagery embody theme and character.

Peter S. Donaldson noted a decade ago that modern Shakespeare directors, staging works written for a bare platform stage,

> must invent a visual design to accompany or supplant the play text. And precisely because words and images, plays and films are so different, study of visual style can often reveal the implicit terms on which Shakespeare and contemporary directors meet.[1]

I too am interested in sites where practitioners may meet, but I take Donaldson's "Shakespeare," in the phrasing of the last sentence, to refer not only to texts, but also to literary ways of looking at texts—the search for images, symbols, and rhetorical strategies. And I aim here to link the activities of the literary critic, who studies dramatic language closely, with those of the film critic, whose concern is with the ways cinematography realizes theme and symbol through mise-en-scene, composition, and montage. Specifically, I want to show how Stuart Burge's directorially conservative *Julius Caesar* (1970) reflects a literary understanding of the play, using as a reference point Maurice Charney's 1961 reading of its verbal and theatrical imagery.

In some respects, my project will seem antiquated. Charney's close readings represent an early period in the history of performance criticism, "when Shakespeare's plays were regarded as poems whose patterns of imagery, both verbal and theatrical, were woven into an organic whole by the 'unitary artistic activity' of the playwright" and when critics searched for "unifying patterns in action, staging, and gesture."[2] Critics who reject the assumptions of that methodology seek, instead, "to discover in performance contingencies more radically destabilizing than anything known to literary critics" (Bulman 1999, 5).

For my present purposes, however, I find it very appropriate to treat the text (or script) of *Julius Caesar* as a unified artifact, grist for close reading, and to deal with the film as a stable performance act. For one thing, Charney's analysis of the imagery in *Julius Caesar* acknowledges the text's systematic ambiguity: it sees Shakespeare's use of images as precise and methodical, but not necessarily "unified." For another, the film industry, by fixing one version of a film as "canonical" through mass distribution, stabilizes performance in ways that cannot happen in live theater.

Cinematography is a very undemocratic discipline, in that it permits audiences only one vantage point per shot and sequence and limits the viewer's visual discretion. The eyes of a theater audience, though influenced by blocking, can nevertheless wander to different points of focus, and each audience member will have a different relationship to the stage, depending on where he or she is seated in the theater. The cinematographer, however, limits what an audience can see and from what angle. If the director wishes to show only a hand, or a ring, or a box in close-up, that is all the camera presents: it permits no other option. There are many philosophies of cinematography, of course, and some compositions are more nondirective than others. In general, however, the camera's ability to determine the vantage point of each audience member stabilizes the cinematic experience.

Technology comes to matter, in this context. The Elizabethans could stage effective storms, helped by gunpowder, thunder sheets, and rolled cannon balls; blood flowed freely. However, the depiction of night scenes was necessarily convention-bound in outdoor theaters, where actors had to indicate the time of day and the condition of the weather by word and gesture. The situation was different in indoor theaters, of course, where artificial light was used; and the later advent of electricity expanded the possibilities for stage lighting enormously. However, film, with its capacity to make vivid the most evanescent of Shakespearean images, its ability to create cinematic meaning through lighting, camera angles, shifting composition, editing, pace, and all the other means at its disposal, can take us many steps further. The art of cinema can employ and modify the art of dramatic poetry.

I want to claim a pedagogical purpose for this essay. Contemporary students, I have found, are generally more adept at appreciating the art of film than the arts of language. Focusing on cinematic language can train minds capable of reacting sensitively to visual signs how to understand the ways of written and spoken language. I want if possible to make a contribution to the restoration of the neglected art of "close reading."

* * *

I must begin by admitting that Burge's *Julius Caesar* is nobody's favorite Shakespeare film. Jack Jorgens dismisses it as "undistinguished," and Jason Robards' listless Brutus is surely an embarrassment to a great actor.[3] Charlton Heston's Antony is imposing, however; John Gielgud's vain Caesar is excellent; and Richard Johnson and Robert Vaughn provide sturdy performances as Cassius and Casca. Indeed, Vaughn's alert eyes make Casca a "point of view" character through which we can scan and judge the actions of others.

Lynda E. Boose and Richard Burt say that Burge's production was "apparently the last instance in which a definably Hollywood film seriously tried to produce Shakespeare straight"—no compliment, from their point of view.[4] Samuel Crowl attributes some of the film's characteristics and strategies to the time of its production, during the Vietnam War, which it perhaps saw from "a postimperialist, postmodern perspective."[5] He cites the opening shots of eagles soaring over battlefields littered with bodies, a cut to a ravaged skull, and a segue to Caesar's triumphant procession. "The film's look and tone and feel reflect its times," and it "seems intentionally ugly" (Crowl 1994, 151).

Indeed, Burge and his director of photography, Ken Higgins, use fairly standard cinematic strategies in their color film, but they do seem to have paid close attention to the play's strands of visual, symbolic, and thematic imagery. I want to "read" their film in relation to Maurice Charney's analysis of the playtext in his 1961 study *Shakespeare's Roman Plays: The Function of Imagery in the Drama*.[6] It is not necessary, I think to argue that Burge and Higgins read Charney and consciously worked his insights into their film; I only note that the filmmakers have found cinematic means to incorporate and deploy Shakespeare's image patterns.

Charney isolates three "chief image themes" in *Julius Caesar*," the storm and its portents, blood, and fire" (1961, 42). Remarking the ways they advance the major themes of *Julius Caesar*, and recognizing the play's complex ambiguities, he notes that each image has "two opposing meanings, depending upon one's point of view" (42):

> With reference to the conspirators, the storm and its portents indicate the evil of Caesar's tyranny in the body politic of Rome, while blood and fire are the means of purging and purifying this evil. But with reference to Caesar and his party, the storm and its portents indicate the evil of conspiracy that is shaking the body politic of Rome, while blood and fire are the signs of assassination and civil strife this evil brings in its wake. (42)

As Charney stresses, the play does not resolve these issues, for while "the defeat and death of the conspirators seems to be a comment on the futility of their enterprise, the rise of Antony and Octavius is by no means an affirmation of justice, truth, and human values" (43). Higgins's cinematography mobilizes Shakespeare's image clusters, while refraining, as the play does, from resolving the issues they invoke in favor of one faction or the other.

The Storm

The storm in *Julius Caesar* manifests itself throughout 1.3, during Cassius's manipulation of Casca, and is alluded to during 2.1 (the conspirators' meeting with Brutus). The storm also forms a link between 2.1 and 2.2 (which takes place at Caesar's residence on the morning of the Ides of March). It is, as usual with Shakespeare, both a natural and a symbolic event. As Charney says, "the imagery of the storm and its portents allows Shakespeare to range freely among the correspondences of man, the state, and the cosmos" (1961, 43)—that is, to elucidate the metaphysical assumptions imbedded in the playtext. "The tempest in nature reflects disturbances in man and the state, or, conversely, these disturbances are projected or externalized in the tempest" (43).

In Burge's film, the storm imagery is registered in sound, as thunder, and visually, as lightning—a white, searing light that slashes the heavens to illuminate Rome and the major characters. We see it first when Cassius, after saying of Caesar, "we will shake him, or worse days endure" (1.2.322), tears a garland from his statue.[7] Lightning and thunder mark a cinematic cut to an evening street scene during which Romans bearing torches scurry for safety from the pelting rain.

The first forty lines of 1.3 are cut, and the scene begins with an altered version of the dialogue between Cassius and Casca ("Who's there?" . . . "A Roman" . . . "Casca, by your voice").

Reversing the playtext's dialogue, Burge turns Casca into a fearful questioner and lets Cassius deliver the line "a Roman" as a sneer at his friend's cowardice. The storm is a portent that Casca fears, whose meaning he questions—"What night is this? Who ever knew the heavens menace so?" (42, 44—lines run together in the screenplay). In response, Cassius offers a confident and self-serving interpretation of events: "Those that have known the earth so full of faults" (45). Cassius enlists the storm in his cause, identifying it and its effects as signs from the heavens, their critical commentary on the rise of Caesar, "A man no mightier than thyself or me / In personal action, yet prodigious grown" (76–77).

Lightning also punctuates the cut to 2.1, which in the film begins with Brutus's rumination "It must be by his death" (2.1.9). By lightning flashes, he reads the parchment thrown in at his door—"Brutus, thou sleep'st" (46)—and lightning punctuates the arrival and introduction of the "faction." The line is cut in the film, but the presence of lightning is indicated by Brutus's comment that "The exhalations whizzing in the air / Give so much light that I may read by them" (2.1.44–45). This observation is something of an afterthought, however: the storm, so devastating in 1.3, is so intermittent that Brutus can observe the stars (2.1.2) and Cinna remark the "gray lines/ That fret the clouds" (103–4).

Though the playtext minimizes the presence of the storm in this scene, the film shows it continuing, if more quietly. Lightning accompanies Casca's lines about the position of sunrise (106–11), to which Burge gives an interesting subtextual twist. This is one of those awkward Shakespearean moments when an action is interrupted to wait for some offstage or upstage event to be completed, leaving the remaining characters to fill the time by chatting among themselves. At its best, such an exigency can generate something marvelous, like Jaques's Seven Ages of Man speech in *As You Like It*; at its worst, it produces the inane dialogue between Escalus and Angelo while they wait for the Duke to shift disguises yet again in 5.1 of *Measure for Measure*.

Here, Cassius has taken Brutus aside to speak of some unspecified matter: "Shall I entreat a word? *They whisper*" (2.1.100). In the meantime, Decius makes a seemingly pointless astronomical inquiry: "Here lies the east. Doth not the day break there?" Casca answers in the negative. "Here, as I point my sword, the sun arises" (106), he says, and, in the playtext goes on for five pedantic lines about the effects of seasonal changes on the location of sunrise ("up higher toward the north/ He first presents his fire" [109–10]). Burge gives the segment great relevance by having Casca point his sword at Brutus when speaking the words "the sun arises," casting him as Rome's savior. At the same moment, another flash of lightning illuminates Brutus.

Is the sword-pointing subtext Shakespearean? I am not sure. It seems an attractive possibility, but then lines 107–11 (which are cut in the film) ramble on too literally afterward. But I accept Burge's cuts and interpolations as valid cinematic emendations that redeem an otherwise clumsy segment.[8] Brutus is the man of the moment, Burge suggests, leaving open the question of whether he is the rising sun or the center of the storm—and if the latter, whether the storm will be cleansing or destructive in its effects.

A flash of lightning, illuminating the very bust from which Cassius tore the decorations at the end of 1.2, also marks the cut to the next scene, a montage of disasters representing Calpurnia's dream. This time, the bust bleeds profusely. (The source scene in the playtext, 2.2, in which Calpurnia describes her dream, starts with the stage direction "*Thunder and lightning.*") The Calpurnia montage, which marks the end of the storm imagery (in playtext and film), foreshadows future events and includes the other major image clusters: the man-made flames of war and riot that follow the assassination, and the shedding of much blood, that of Caesar, the mob, and soldiers in combat.

In playtext and film, the storm is related to Cassius's scheming and Brutus's mortal torment. With the resolution of these issues in the minds of the protagonists—when Brutus has decided to join the assassins, and Caesar has decided he will go to the Senate—the natural storm vanishes as a motif. Except for the appearance of Caesar's ghost, the heavens do not concern themselves with the fates or choices of men beyond that point. The human storm, the rioting mob that burns and vandalizes, becomes the instrument of fear and destruction.

Fire

Charney remarks that the play's fire imagery also has dual meanings, depending on one's attitude toward the rebellion. On the one hand, fire symbolizes passion and emotional power (of the sort kindled by Antony in his oration). On the other hand, it functions as a destructive and purifying force: "This is the literal sense of fire, and it is carried into the stage action when the mob which Antony has inflamed lights firebrands to burn the conspirators' houses" (Charney 1961, 60).

Burge and Higgins certainly employ fire in these ways, as we shall see, but they use it in other ways as well. The red glow of domestic fire accompanies moments of family intimacy, as when Portia (Diana Rigg), sitting at Brutus's feet, pleads to be let into his confidence. Calpurnia (Jill Bennett) will later adopt the same posture when dissuading Caesar from going to the Senate. Both women, by the glow of domestic light, earnestly seek to know their husbands' hearts and protect them from harm. However, when Antony and Octavius (Richard Chamberlain) compose their list of those who will die in the wake of their victory, they do so by a harsher torchlight (while being massaged in a bathhouse). Similar lighting, originating in torchlight but lacking the warmth of the hearth, accompanies the quarrel of Brutus and Cassius before Philippi.

In the public arena, however, fire is generally destructive, signaling passion, riot and ruin. The domestic and public functions of fire are nicely combined when Brutus reads the parchments thrown in at his door at Cassius's suggestion. As mentioned earlier, Brutus begins to read by lightning, but Higgins and Burge contrive that Robards hold the message at such an angle that flame from a household torch seems to emanate from it. In the context of Brutus's home, the orange flame has domestic connotations, but the composition of the shot simultaneously suggests the inflammatory nature of the message Brutus reads.

Marc Antony's oration takes place in full daylight, but in the area in which he speaks, outside the Senate, many standing torches are placed, visually punctuating his impassioned words. Having enraged the crowd, Antony walks among the flames as the rioting Romans bear torches to cremate Caesar and then burn down the homes of the conspirators. As the mob races madly through the streets, fire becomes their instrument of vengeance and manifests vividly the destructive power of their passions. Finally, the ghost of Caesar speaks to Brutus through the flickering, orange flame of a candle, promising to be his "evil spirit" at Philippi (4.3.283).

Blood

Blood imagery, verbal and visual, lends itself easily to cinematic treatment. As Charney points out, "Caesar's bloody and rent body is on stage" throughout much of 3.1 and 3.2; it "dominates the scene for almost 450 lines after his death"; and it "plays a conspicuous role during Antony's funeral oration." Blood serves, thereby, "as a visible indictment of the conspirators" (Charney 1961, 52), and is the focus of Marc Antony's successful effort to turn the crowd from their initial admiration of Brutus to a vengeful indignation over the death of Caesar.

Blood imagery makes its first appearance in the film as a screaming Calpurnia awakes from her dream of Caesar's statue spouting blood (2.2 of the playtext). We also see, in montage, a flash-forward of events to come: Artemidorus's effort to warn Caesar of the plot; scenes of the war and devastation that will follow the assassination; and rioting crowds bearing torches.

Though it disappears for a while, blood imagery is violently revived in 3.1 at the assassination itself and used thereafter to keep the event ever before the mind of the audience. As Charney notes (Charney 1961, 52), Shakespeare employs verbal irony here: surrounded by pretended petitioners who intend to stab him, Caesar declares that he will not be moved by pleadings that "might fire the blood of ordinary men" (3.1.38); that he does not bear "such rebel blood" (3.1.41) as to be moved by persuasion.

As the conspirators in the film surround Caesar and methodically plunge their daggers into his body, blood freely floods his garments and splashes on his face. Seeking rescue, Caesar staggers toward Brutus, whose back is to him. Brutus at last turns to face Caesar, shakes off his hand, and then, to Caesar's shock and amazement, draws his dagger against him and plunges it in as Caesar collapses in a bloody heap after "*Et tu, Brutè?* Then fall Caesar" (3.1.78).

Charney remarks that in the Globe staging of the conspirators' act of bathing their hands in Caesar's wounds, "stage blood was liberally used . . . since the conspirator's hands and swords need to remain very vividly bloody for about 150 lines" (Charney 1961, 52). Convinced of their cause, their eyes "on posterity, which they are sure will approve their present acts," the bloody-handed conspirators reach at that moment "the highest point in [their] development" (53):

> . . . Let us bathe our hands in Caesar's blood
> Up to the elbows and besmear our swords.
> Then walk we forth even to the marketplace,
> And, waving our red weapons 'o'er our heads,
> Let's all cry "Peace, freedom, and liberty."
>   (3.1.107–11)

Their bloody hands and swords they intend as "visual signs they now flaunt to all Rome as justification of their deed" (Charney 1961, 54).

The film lets us understand immediately that this gesture will not work as intended. An overhead shot shows the conspirators staining their hands. Proud to declare and demonstrate their connections to the assassination, the conspirators nevertheless create an awkward physical situation for themselves. Blood is sticky, messy stuff. As they hold their hands palms-outward, so as not to stain their clothes, the conspirators in some *gestural* sense repudiate their deed even as they praise it. As Charlton Heston's Antony shakes the hands of each conspirator in the film, the audience is further reminded of the physical properties of blood—its thickness and viscosity.

By contrast to the conspirators and their body language, however, Marc Antony eagerly marks himself with the blood he seeks to avenge. Charney offers the rationale for that view: "Antony's speeches in this scene reiterate 'blood' both as the symbol of the murdered Caesar and as the sign of the conspirators' guilt" (Charney 1961, 53).

> O pardon me, thou bleeding piece of earth,
> That I am meek and gentle with these butchers!
> Thou art the ruins of the noblest man
> That ever lived in the tide of times.
> Woe to the hand that shed this costly blood!
> Over thy wounds now do I prophesy—
> Which, like dumb mouths, do ope their ruby lips
> To beg the voice and utterance of my tongue—
> A curse shall light upon the limbs of men;
> Domestic fury and fierce civil strife
> Shall cumber all the parts of Italy;
> Blood and destruction shall be so in use
> And dreadful objects so familiar
> That mothers shall but smile when they behold

> Their infants quartered with the hands of war,
> All pity choked with custom of fell deeds;
> And Caesar's spirit, ranging for revenge
> Shall in these confines with a monarch's voice
> Cry havoc and let slip the dogs of war.
>
> (3.1.256–75)

Heston, after declaring Caesar "the noblest man / That ever lived in the tide of times" (258–59), deliberately slips his own hand into one of Caesar's wounds. At "Over thy wounds now do I prophesy" (261), he holds his hands palm-downward; he picks up Caesar's very dead hand at "the hand of war" (268); and he deliberately rubs it against his mouth at the word "havoc" (273). The blood that smears Charlton Heston's face reinforces the idea that wounds speak, that blood is eloquent and compels revengeful action.

At his funeral oration, Antony uses Caesar's mantle to outrage the crowd, identifying each hole in it with the conspirator who made it, loudly ripping the cloth as he indicates where "the well beloved Brutus stabbed" (3.2.176), and, finally, after turning up the face of a weeping mourner, exposing his bloody corpse itself with a sweeping gesture at "Look you here, / Here is himself, marred as you see with traitors" (197–98). As Antony precludes any rebuttal by predicting to the now frantic crowd that the "wise and honorable" conspirators will "no doubt with reasons" answer his accusations, we see Casca and Cinna slink away.

After this, the crowd riots, plucking down "benches . . . forms, windows, anything" (258–59), burning, looting, and racing madly about. They carry Caesar's body on the run to burn it "in the holy place" (254) and bear torches to fire the houses of Brutus and Cassius. The film cuts the killing of Cinna the Poet, but a quick sight of a body trampled by the rampaging mob visually represents the evil of mindless violence.

* * *

We have long stopped thinking of the theatrical as the enemy of the literary, in relation to Shakespeare: instead, we celebrate the ways the disciplines enhance each other. My suggestion here has been that we expand our performance vocabulary by developing more and richer ways to use film in our criticism and in our pedagogy. While I don't suppose I have made any converts to Burge's film, and did not intend to, I hope I have suggested ways to bring to bear upon the study of "Shakespeare" (conceived textually, theatrically, or cinematically) more of the resources at our command, and to equip our students to understand more deeply the possibilities offered by new media and old.

Notes

1. Donaldson, Peter S., ed. 1990. *Shakespearean Films/Shakespearean Directors*. Boston: Unwin Hyman, xii.

2. Bulman, James C. 1999. "Shakespeare and Performance Theory." In *Shakespeare, Theory, and Performance*, edited by James C. Bulman. New York: Routledge, 5.

3. Jorgens, Jack. 1977. *Shakespeare on Film*. Bloomington: Indiana University Press, 2.

4. Boose, Lynda E., and Richard Burt. 1997. "Totally Clueless?" In *Shakespeare the Movie: Popularizing the Plays on Film, TV, and Video*, edited by Lynda E. Boose and Richard Burt. New York: Routledge, 13.

5. Crowl, Samuel. 1994. "The Roman Plays on Film and Television." In *Shakespeare and the Moving Image: The Plays on Film and Television*, edited by Anthony Davies and Stanley Wells. Cambridge: Cambridge University Press, 151.

6. Charney, Maurice. 1961. *Shakespeare's Roman Plays: The Function of Imagery in the Drama*. Cambridge: Harvard University Press.

7. Citations from the play are to Bevington, David, ed. 1992. *The Complete Works of Shakespeare*. Fourth edition. New York: HarperCollins Publishers.

8. It well may be that this staging has a production history of which I am unaware.

Teaching What's Not There

ALAN C. DESSEN

IN ADAPTING SHAKESPEARE'S PLAYS FOR LATE-TWENTIETH-CENTURY AUDIences directors make many adjustments in order to 1) streamline the playscript and save running time by cutting speeches or entire scenes, 2) eliminate the obscurity caused by mythological allusions, difficult syntax, and archaic words, 3) conserve on personnel by eliminating figures completely (Lovell in *Richard III*) or telescoping together various lesser characters, 4) sidestep stage practices appropriate to the Globe that might mystify today's playgoer or actor, and occasionally 5) cancel out a passage that might not fit comfortably with a particular agenda or "concept."[1] Such decisions yield practical and sometimes conceptual gains but also involve some losses or diminutions, so my rhetoric includes repeated references to what I term *price tags* and *trade-offs*, both the pluses and minuses of a director's *rescripting* or *re*[play]*wrighting*.

 I will focus upon moments in productions of six plays available on videocassette. In addition, at the risk of seeming perverse I will single out and discuss items omitted from these productions so as to show how such omissions can generate fruitful problems for the classroom. In foregrounding such choices my purpose is *not* to snipe at directors and actors but to suggest how such rescripting or reimaging can be put to use by the teacher.

 My first example is a half-line omitted from the Thames Television version of Trevor Nunn's Royal Shakespeare Company production of *Macbeth* (5.1.53) where after Lady Macbeth's "O,O,O!" the doctor in the full script reacts "What a sigh is there! The heart is sorely charg'd," but the director omits the first five words.[2] Here Judi Dench turns the three Os into perhaps the most powerful single moment in a very powerful show, a horrible scream that my students link to a soul damned in hell. Only the rare purist among those students questions this cut when I note it, for to include the doctor's "What a sigh is there!" would run the risk of trivializing or otherwise undercutting this moment. I do regularly call attention to the omission, however, both as an excellent example of the give-and-take relationship between the received Folio script and today's theatrical choices and as a way of posing the unanswerable question: what constitutes a "legitimate" omission from the script?

My second example is from director Nicholas Hytner's Lincoln Center production of *Twelfth Night* shown on PBS on 30 August 1998. Of the many cuts or other rescriptings in this show the most suggestive to me was the omission of a Malvolio line from the letter or box-tree scene (2.5.166–67) where, after reading the letter supposedly from Olivia, he comments: "She did commend my yellow stockings of late, she did praise my leg being cross-garter'd." As with the omission of the doctor's half-line, the director's rationale is clear, for later in this scene Maria tells the other conspirators that "He will come to her in yellow stockings, and 'tis a color she abhors, and cross-garter'd, a fashion she detests" (2.5.198–200). To omit Malvolio's supposed "memory" is therefore to eliminate an anomaly, a possible source of confusion. When would Malvolio have worn such an outlandish outfit? Given Maria's comment, how could Olivia have commended or praised it?"

However, for the teacher of this scene the director's omission can generate a fruitful discussion about a rationale for the anomaly and perhaps reasons why it should be left in, even stressed. With or without reference to recent controversies about recovered (and perhaps bogus) memories, one can argue that Maria's explanation is given such a climactic placement to cause a reader or playgoer to reassess just how far Malvolio has gone or will go to hold on to his pipe dream or delusional vision that he is Olivia's beloved. Noting the director's omission has generated some good classroom discussions of Malvolio's mind set and the scene as a whole.

Given the enormous textual problems facing an editor or director of *Hamlet*, to delve into comparable script choices in this playscript is to fall into a bottomless pit. Rather than ignore this play completely, however, I will include one small example—if only for comic relief. The 1979 BBC-TV production, directed by Rodney Bennett with Derek Jacobi as Hamlet, has many virtues, one of which is the ghost as played by Patrick Allen, so that I regularly use in my classes this show's rendition of 1.4 and 1.5. The closet scene is another matter, however, for although I like the camera work and the use of sound to distinguish adroitly between what Hamlet and Gertrude see and hear, this production is one of the few in recent memory to costume the ghost in act 3 in the armor of act 1. Those knowledgeable about the muddied textual situation will know that in the first (or supposedly "bad") quarto the ghost enters in a nightgown (and therefore is clearly differentiated from act 1) whereas the second quarto and the Folio provide no such specific signal. In the dialogue in both the "good" texts, however, Hamlet describes to Gertrude the departure "out at the portal" of "My father, in his habit as he lived!" (3.4.135–36). If I do show this scene in class, I ask my students: can you conjure up a marital relationship wherein the husband regularly wears armor when visiting his wife? One scenario is that Gertrude may have been so sexually rapacious that Hamlet senior needed the protection. Perhaps your students can come up with better answers.

To move to more substantive matters, the 1953 Hollywood *Julius Caesar* directed by Joseph Mankiewicz makes many revealing cuts. For me the most interesting omission comes just after the assassination of Caesar (3.1.105–11). Here the director gives us what I think of as the antiseptic approach to this scene, with limited stage blood for the murder (enhanced by the absence of color) and then a paring back of the ritual over Caesar's body. In the director's rescripting, Brutus says: "Stoop, Romans, stoop, / and let us bathe our hands in Caesar's blood," and these lines are followed by Cassius's "How many ages hence" speech and the two subsequent speeches from Brutus and Cassius, followed by a brief (and unrevealing) kneeling around the body. What is omitted is:

> *Brutus.*   [Stoop, Romans, stoop,
>   And let us bathe our hands in Caesar's blood]
>   Up to the elbows, and besmear our swords;
>   Then walk we forth, even to the marketplace,
>   And waving our red weapons o'er our heads,
>   Let's all cry, "Peace, freedom, and liberty!"
> *Cassius.* Stoop then, and wash.
>   (3-1)

In contrast, the 1978 BBC-TV production directed by Herbert Wise provides both a brutal assassination and so much blood in the bathing up to the elbows that later in the scene Antony's hands are also visibly reddened after the series of handshakes.

The staging choices in the 1953 production are integrally entwined with a long standing though now unfashionable interpretation built around Brutus as a noble Roman who unlike the other conspirators, is untainted by these events and therefore remains throughout the play an embodiment of admirable qualities and principles. This interpretation has not fared well in recent decades, a victim of various forces including what has been termed the hermeneutics of suspicion. In setting up the problem for my students, I start with the orchard scene where Brutus, in presenting his case not to kill Antony, argues:

> Let us be sacrificers, but not butchers, Caius.
> We all stand up against the spirit of Caesar,
> And in the spirit of men there is no blood;
> O that we then could come by Caesar's spirit,
> And not dismember Caesar! But, alas,
> Caesar must bleed for it! And, gentle friends,
> Let's kill him boldly, but not wrathfully;
> Let's carve him as a dish fit for the gods,
> Not hew him as a carcass fit for hounds;
> (2.1.266–74)

Both in the assassination and its aftermath staging choices can determine whether a viewer see a sacrifice or a butchery, a carving or a hewing, a bold or a wrathful action, or (later in the same speech) a purging or a murder (2.1.180). To omit any ritual bathing in Caesar's blood is to omit a potentially powerful, even nauseating image wherein bloody hands "Up to the elbows" and bloody swords can provide a disturbing theatrical counterpoint to words such as "Peace, freedom, and liberty" and can strongly affect what follows. For example, when Antony offers love and friendship "Upon this hope, that you shall give me reasons / Why, and wherein, Caesar was dangerous," Brutus responds "Or else were this a savage spectacle" (3.1.220–22). This response resonates very differently in the 1953 version, where both the assassination and the aftermath lack visible savagery, as opposed to the BBC and other recent stagings that display plentiful blood. The noble Brutus or noble Romans approach is much easier to sustain with the Mankiewicz cuts and related choices, so that using segments from two contrasting productions has generated some fruitful discussions in my classes about conceptual rescripting.[3]

Comparable omissions that facilitate a particular interpretation turn up regularly. For example, in *The Merchant of Venice* a viewer should not be surprised to find some or all of Shylock's aside in his first scene (1.3.41–52) gone in production, especially the comment

"If I can catch him once upon the hip, / I will feed fat the ancient grudge I bear him" (46–47), for this passage suggests to some readers and theatrical professionals a long range plan that does not mesh comfortably with prevailing interpretations. For example, in the cinematic version of Jonathan Miller's production, Laurence Olivier provides an extended display of a moment of revelation in 3.1 (the equivalent to a light bulb going off in his head) when the notion of enforcing the bond of flesh comes to him. That interpretation (that Shylock only decides to go for the pound of flesh after the elopement of Jessica) is possible without omitting all or part of the earlier aside, but the Miller–Olivier approach is definitely enhanced when that earlier expression of intent is cut. To argue in a classroom the pros and cons of the aside is also to get involved with questions of iterative imagery: how does the loss of "feed fat the ancient grudge I bear him" affect "to bait fish withal" (3.1.53) or other feeding imagery that permeates the play up through the trial scene? If the line referring to the hip ("If I can catch him once upon the hip") is gone from the aside in 1.3, what effect does that omission have on our understanding of Gratiano's line after the reversal in act 4 ("Now, infidel, I have you on the hip"—4.1.334)?

The two highly visible cinema versions of *Romeo and Juliet* (directed by Franco Zeffirelli in 1968 and Baz Luhrmann in 1996) provide many suggestive examples, for both directors omit huge chunks of the original script. For example, neither includes Romeo's killing of Paris in the final scene. Ironically, this omission is a reversion to the plot as presented in Shakespeare's source, Arthur Brooke's *Romeus and Juliet,* so that both Zeffirelli and Luhrmann leave out what Shakespeare chose to add to the received story. For me, however, the most suggestive cut is found in the two renditions of Juliet's taking of the potion (4.3.14–58). In both film scenes the movement to this key action is very fast, with the emphasis upon visual effects and music, not dialogue.

Some of the logic behind this choice may be linked to the limitations of the actress, in particular Zeffirelli's Olivia Hussey. But I find these cinematic choices *very* useful in teaching this play, for citing this omission has led to fruitful discussions of this long and potentially significant speech. At first many of my students approve of the abbreviated cinematic versions, for, given their reflexes and ingrained sense of narrative pacing, they do not relish forty "what if" lines from Juliet and therefore, at least initially, prefer the combination of music and "cut to the chase" plotting. But a reading aloud in class of the speech, with an emphasis upon the horrors conjured up by the heroine that provide a context for her final "I drink to thee," can provide an effective counterargument. The most successful Juliets I have seen (and that list does not include Olivia Hussey and Claire Danes) have made this speech the heart of their interpretation, the moment when Juliet attains a stature granted to no one else in the play, including Romeo. For me and for many actresses, the series of potential horrors detailed in the *what ifs* is essential to conveying the difficulty of her choice and the courage needed to make it. In this instance, I argue that a production of this script that omits this speech can still be a moving and highly enjoyable romantic melodrama but loses any claim to being a presentation of Shakespeare's Juliet. For me, this cut constitutes not rescripting but rewrighting.

Finally (and most complexly) I will end with one of the most challenging scenes in the canon, the banquet scene in *Macbeth*. Of the many potential issues here worthy of exploration, I have found most fruitful in pedagogical terms the question: should or should not the ghost be visible to the viewer as well as to Macbeth? In my experience, a large majority of stage productions retain the two appearances of a visible ghost as scripted in the Folio, but cinema-television renditions vary widely. For example, in his film version director Roman Polanski provides a visible ghost but rescripts the scene so as to have one continuous sequence, not an exit and a reentrance. The Eric Porter-Janet Suzman television production presents the Folio ghost, but the Nicol Williamson-Jane Lapotaire BBC-TV version does not. Certainly the most powerful rendition of a nonvisible ghost is found in the Trevor Nunn RSC production already cited.

Here I find myself badly conflicted, for my theater historian gene strongly supports the Folio reading, whereas the Trevor Nunn rendition, especially what I take to be the punch line (Ian McKellen's rendition of "I am a man again" with saliva dripping from a clenched jaw), is very effective. Admittedly, there are many ways to interpret the differences between the two approaches, for much will depend upon one's reading of other parts of the play (e.g., the witches). My own formulation for the classroom is keyed to what I take to be a defining moment in the play, the "what man dare" speech (3.4.98–107) which for me boils down to the statement: I can handle anything but this sight. I therefore frame the question for my students: what exactly is it that Macbeth cannot face?

Not surprisingly, students and actors today are most comfortable with some form of psychological realism, an approach in this instance keyed to a Macbeth who is wrestling with what appear to be internal demons rather than a Macbeth who is confronted with a supernatural entity. The majority of my students therefore prefer a ghost only visible to Macbeth so that the X which he cannot face is something within himself, a reading that fits neatly with other passages in the script—for example, "To know my deed, 'twere best not know myself" (2.2.70). The Folio, which signals two entrances for the ghost, clearly calls for an actor to play a visible and usually bloody Banquo ("never shake / Thy gory locks at me"—3.4.49–50) who takes Macbeth's seat once and sometimes twice (as in the Porter-Suzman version where John Thaw's Banquo sits on a throne at the second entrance). An onstage ghost does not rule out a psychological reading but, unlike a figure only seen by Macbeth, can allow or encourage a sense of a supernatural entity in keeping with the witches, the apparitions, and a possible satanic pronunciation of S-E-Y-T-O-N. As I like to pose the question: is Macbeth unable to confront something in himself (or what he has become) or is he unable to confront something that exists outside the world of man and therefore beyond the capabilities of even a hero who can triumph over "the rugged Russian bear, / The arm'd rhinoceros, or th'Hyrcan tiger"? Statements such as "What man dare, I dare" and "I am a man again" clearly echo other passages in the tragedy that link manhood with *dare-do-deed* and, at least with Macduff, with feeling ("But I must also feel it as a man"—4.3221). McKellen's presentation of a Macbeth who is subhuman, something less than a man, at the climax of this speech sets up powerfully how far he has descended and fits smoothly with a ghost linked to his internal demons, but the alternative reading can be just as powerful and meaningful if what the tragic protagonist cannot combat comes from beyond this little world of man.

In conclusion, my examples culled from six plays vary considerably in significance and complexity, but each can be useful in the classroom for posing questions or making distinctions. Is the omission of Malvolio's supposed memory of Olivia's praise an elimination of a source of confusion, hence a smoothing out of a Shakespeare muddle? Or does the change cancel out a meaningful signal so that a scripted effect is diminished? The 1953 Mankiewicz cuts in the assassination scene are far less likely to be found today, for the interpretative stance they support is out of fashion (readers and directors now *prefer* blood and savagery), but to doctor somehow the acting script of *The Merchant of Venice* so as to yield a more sympathetic Shylock (as in director David Thacker's 1993 RSC stage production) remains standard practice. Using these or comparable examples in the classroom can bring into focus the scope available to the theatrical professional as interpreter. Similarly, only the rare stage production will omit Juliet's 4.3 soliloquy, but the absence of this speech in two widely seen and much discussed movies provides a good point of departure for dealing with a variety of issues that include the links between key choices and tragic stature and the pros and cons of poetic-verbal complexity. Most tellingly, I have found that debates about the visible or nonvisible ghost in the banquet scene have generated fruitful insights into my students' often unacknowledged assumptions about the supernatural, states of mind, choice, and even politics.

Raising questions about the words to be spoken or omitted inevitably gets the teacher involved with murky editorial and textual problems. I confess that I have not had great success, at least with undergraduates, in dealing with the instabilities in various Shakespeare texts, whether the two versions of *King Lear* or the vagaries of *Hamlet* or *Othello*, an area of investigation that appeals to me but not to my clientele. Moreover, my students, who are anything but textual purists, often approve of directors who take liberties with the original words and sequence of scenes and therefore prefer cinematic versions such as the Parker-Fishburne-Branagh *Othello* or the Branagh *Much Ado About Nothing* that streamline the original playscripts and invoke various television or cinematic conventions with which they are familiar. To such students playing pedagogical games linked to "what's not there?" can seem artificial or, in a pejorative sense, "academic."

My response is to invoke something akin to truth in advertising. I, for one, will pay close attention to any theatrical interpretation that is based on a reading of the received playscript, but, in the spirit of consumerism, I pose a series of questions. When situated in a text-based English literature classroom, what is the appropriate stance for evaluating stage or cinematic productions of Shakespeare's plays? More specifically, how are we to evaluate a reading or staging that to sustain its interpretation must omit or ignore a significant part of the original text? On a spectrum that ranges from the second quarto of *Romeo and Juliet* to *West Side Story*, at what point does one move from interpretation to translation or rewrighting? Should we, as teachers and students, care about such matters? If not us, then who?

To belabor a point, whether in this collection, in the classroom, or in writing essays on performance history, I have no interest in what I think of as the Blame Game, the academic process of fault finding wherein the director becomes a vandal sacking the sacred text. Rather, my goal is to single out directorial or actorly choices and then explore the implications of those choices for interpretation. Since Shakespeare did not script his plays with us in mind, such an approach is inevitably intertwined with cultural differences in one form or another whether those differences are attached to assumptions about ghosts and the supernatural, as in the banquet scene, or my students' sense of narrative (and their impatience with poetry) as opposed to the demonstrable assets of complex poetry and iterative imagery. To single out repeatedly for discussion elements that are absent from a production is to flirt with various dangers (e.g., academic snideness, artificiality), but, as I have sought to demonstrate, I have found various pedagogical advantages in this approach, particularly in generating discussions about key moments such as the assassination of Caesar, Juliet's potion-taking, and Macbeth's dilemma in the banquet scene. To borrow from Mark Antony, not to explore such avenues would be "the most unkindest cut of all" (3.2.183).

Notes

1. Citations from Shakespeare are taken from the Riverside edition, Evans, G. Blakemore. 1974. Boston: Houghton Mifflin.

2. The 1999 production of London's new Globe Theater directed by Mark Rylance also did not include a bathing up to the elbows in blood, presumably because the actors were wearing long sleeved Elizabethan costumes. A substantial amount of blood *was* visible, however, on both Caesar's body in 3.2 and the ghost in 4.3.

The New Globe

Pauline Kiernan

It is a building built at the turn of the twentieth century but its design is based on principles that are four centuries old. It is constructed with green, unseasoned (and, therefore in effect, still "living") oak timbers. The roof is made with a water reed thatch, to Tudor specifications as far as modern safety regulations require. Sprinklers positioned round the tip of the thatch are designed to prevent a repetition of the theater burning down as it did during a performance of *Henry VIII* on 29 June 1613. Experiments have demonstrated that a fire at the new Globe can be extinguished in minutes. That invaluable provider of unique knowledge about the early modern theater, the Swiss visitor Sir Thomas Platter, called it "The house with the thatched roof," and archaeologists found quantities of water reed at the Rose excavations just across the road from the Globe's original site, in 1989, so it is probable that the Globe used the same kind of thatch.[1] The new Globe is supported by wooden pegs, and its three hundred feet of wall is plastered with lime and goats' hair by means of a technique that goes back to 2,400 B.C.[2]

I have begun with a physical description of the new Globe because the reconstructed building has allowed—or prompted—us to concentrate on the *physical* conditions of the configuration of actors and audience, stage and auditorium, and the dramaturgical implications of this physical, material relationship.

Actors who have been used to delivering Shakespeare's language on a proscenium arch stage to a largely invisible audience who are seated in a darkened auditorium say that it is the physical characteristics of the open-air theater that seem to make the words count for almost "everything." What interests me about their emphasis on the text, the words, the prose, the verse, the rhythms in a Shakespeare play as being foregrounded in this way, is that the spoken word is made to carry so much of the weight of the play. As one of the actors said: "There's no lighting, no technology to help you, so you are thrown back on the plays. The words tell the audience what is small, what is big."

Just as significant, I think, is the way that the open amphitheater encourages "moving on the line." If you stand still for any length of time on the stage, the energy goes. The space loves movement. One of the significant implications of this, of course, has to do with speed of performance. Rather than stop, say the line, move, stop, say the line, the actor literally moves while delivering the lines. Perhaps now the "two hours' traffic" in a Shakespeare text, which has prompted so much debate, begins to sound rather less implausible.

When the academic and architectural advisors first planned the reconstructed Globe, they assumed that the stage was bathed in sunlight, and its audience conveniently cast in the shade. Solving the problem of the theater's orientation on the site required turning the building round, with the surprising discovery that the stage always remained in the shade.[3] Instead of the actors being in the "spotlight," then, it is the playgoers who are highly visible, to the actors on stage and, most significantly, to one another. The seemingly simple fact of the building's orientation affects every aspect of the theater experience. Daylight falls on everything in this space. With no elaborate set design, without controlled lighting to direct and control the audience's attention, the stage requires the actors to work harder to draw the audience into a fictitious world, which makes it easier for the playgoers to become actively absorbed in the story. If there is no artificial lighting on the stage, what the audience hears often becomes more important than what it sees. The furthest distance between a playgoer and the actor at the center of the stage is about fifty feet. In a packed house, actors on the new Globe stage are surrounded by 1500–1700 playgoers on three sides—four sides if there are playgoers in the balcony.

The traditional reason for there being so few stage directions in Shakespeare's plays, that he was on hand to "direct" the stage, may be less important than two other factors: the aural signals within the text which have to do so much work in creating mood, establishing location and describing action; and the fixed physical structure, the architectural characteristics of the stage which present limitations to staging and blocking but also offer effective dramaturgical possibilities. The echoing of verbal patterns and the modulating of reiterated images throughout a scene or a whole play necessarily become more pronounced and therefore of greater dramaturgical significance.

A central opening, flanked by two entry doors, demands to be used not only for exits and entrances, but for concealment, for eavesdropping and, of course, for discovery. So far, experience of using the central opening as a discovery space has proved problematic at the new Globe because a large part of the audience, and playgoers' in the lords' room above the stage, cannot see what is happening in the space. With the production of *The Winter's Tale* in 1997, the company experimented in the rehearsal room with where to place Hermione's "statue." It was decided she would stand beneath the "fiery cloud" in the heavens inside a circular curtain hanging from a hoop held up by attendants, at about the same spot where she had stood for trial inside a cage in 2.1. The actors stood around her to minimize the risk of playgoers seeing the "statue" breathing. Michael Gould, who played Polixenes, felt that the scene is written in such a way that the audience does not need to see the statue, that the audience gets everything it needs from the words: "I wish in retrospect we had been braver and not gone for the visual thing, that we had trusted the language, and put Hermione in the discovery space. There are so many lines dedicated to what is happening, and if the audience can see it anyway, it makes the lines redundant."

Every actor I have interviewed who has played the new Globe stage emphasized that the theater is a *listening* space. Voice coach Jeanette Nelson thinks that "acoustically, the theater feels very resonant and actors hear their voices coming back to them. For the audience to be engaged with what the actor's saying, the actors need to use their training and skills to the full. It isn't a question of volume. It's to do with giving clarity to the word." Actor David Fielder, who played Llewellyn in *Henry V*, says, "You don't have to shout, it can be very gentle. Clarity is important, you can pull it in quite small, the sound. You have to listen to the audience, know when to give time to their responses." When actors talk of the theater being a listening space, they mean actors as well as playgoers have to listen. Jeanette Nelson is again helpful here: "Using the voice in the modern way—we tend to let the sound go away at the end of sentences—does not work. In the new Globe, actors have to complete the ends of their words and sentences." This has proved particularly important for being able to hear your cue backstage. David Fielder says, "It's a question of passing on the energy at the end of the line, certainly at the end of a scene. You have to end the line at the right pitch—it's as though you're passing the baton." Actor and artistic director Mark Rylance believes aural story telling is the medium for everything in this theater. "Thoughts are experienced within a human emotional context more powerfully in this amphitheater architecture than in a proscenium design." He thinks "this may have to do with the heavier dependance on sound and hearing as a medium rather than vision and sight," and he's noticed that "the emotional experience for an audience is both individual and collective at the same time." His views on the theater's physical effects on the actor are particularly interesting: "The physical activeness of the body whether standing or seated at the new Globe is a quite different state for the heart and mind. The elements add to an awakened, sometimes drenched, sense of the physical body." Actor William Russell, who played the King of France in *Henry V*, says: "It's what the audience *hear* that they react to. And they do hear, I've watched the audience listening, and *I'm* listening in a new way to the other actors on the stage."

One of the interesting discoveries of the first seasons was actors' responses to delivering soliloquies in the space. Matthew Scurfield, who played the Duke in *The Two Gentlemen of Verona* in the prologue season, Exeter in *Henry V* and Yellowhammer in *A Chaste Maid in Cheapside*, both in the opening season, thinks that they

> become a very sharing thing, considering that it's very private as well. Although you're talking to 1500 people on your own it feels really private and secret, and the playgoer feels the actor is talking to him/her as an individual. Having worked here, it's so obvious now that a soliloquy has to be shared with the audience. To let us, the audience, into the play, to bring us to that situation, to make us more involved. As an actor, you realize you can't deliver soliloquies to yourself.

Scurfield's view may not put an end to scholarly debate about who soliloquies are supposed to be delivered to, but an actor's experience of playing a twentieth-century reconstruction of a sixteenth-century playhouse will need now to be taken into account in any discussion of the subject.

Maureen Beattie, who appeared in *Damon and Pythias* in the prologue season, thinks the space demands, vocally, the old art of "*projection*," the ability to send the words and emotions out to the audience without shouting or losing subtlety.

Sonia Ritter, who played Nerissa in *The Merchant of Venice* and Infelice in *The Honest Whore*, both 1998 season, says that rehearsing a play in the rehearsal room, "you have massively to adapt to the bare stage." She is particularly helpful on the question of the physical effect of the space on the language: "Language," she thinks, "has to be physicalised, not exaggerated to fill the space. The old language and ideas that are so called obscure or considered on the fringe of our contemporary vocabulary will take flight upon the emotion." She adds: "The integrity that the actors must devote themselves to is the committing to the language of his/her character. We live in an age of enormously abstract theater. We're afraid of the old language, but by speaking the text, rather than describing it, you make it live on stage."

Movement coach Sue Lefton says: "In more conventional theaters all of the focus of the audience is on the stage, the lighting, the elaborate set. At the new Globe, it's the actor, the text and the audience. The actor's body has more demands made on it; you cannot separate the physical from the text. The Globe doesn't respond to "greyness": it responds to strong definition. Basically it encourages a movement that culminates in a larger physical expression that has to be very clear, that is not always naturalistic, but which is definitely not grand gestures. Sonia Ritter says: "In the modern theater we can get locked into a need to analyze, so that the ideas are coming into the preparation before we let the text do its work. We need to go for the blood and muscle, not the brain: to inhabit the verse, the prose, that's the play. It's you and the text. Picking up a Shakespeare text is like going into a gymnasium—you have to flex *every* muscle."

Andrew French, who played Gratiano in *Merchant* and Lodovico Sforza in *The Honest Whore*, thinks that verse in the new Globe "compels people to listen." Clarence Smith, who played Lorenzo in *Merchant* and Matheo in *Honest Whore*, says, "It is the texture of the space that allows you to communicate thought directly to the audience."

It is too soon to know yet in how many ways our experiences of voices in a reconstructed Globe theater are going to inform aspects of Shakespeare scholarship. If we concentrate on the physical effects of the new theater, on the purely physical playing of the plays, we may be better equipped to conjecture on the physical effects of the original building. It would seem, though, that the physical propensities of an open air wooden amphitheater where the actor is the center of a circle of playgoers suggest that what original audiences at

Shakespeare's plays *heard* was often more important than what they *saw*.

There is, of course, the vexed question of original audiences. It is impossible—indeed, undesirable—to historicize them. For one thing, the maximum capacity at the original theater is believed to have been about 3,000, in comparison to the new Globe's 1,500–1,700. This must affect every aspect of a study of the new Globe and its possible relationship with the old. And this begs the question, can the reconstructed theater tells us anything about the original playhouse? Even if we were able to telescope time in the way Shakespeare so adeptly did, shrink our bodies to the smaller bulk of an Elizabethan adult, replace our twentieth-century mind-sets with sixteenth-century ones, could we hope to "become" Elizabethans (if we wanted to do so)? Exploring "authentic" staging practices proves problematic, not least because we have relatively little knowledge of what these staging practices were. What are we to make of the 1999 Globe production of *Julius Caesar* featuring Elizabethans playing Romans? Or the plebeians emerging from the yard in baseball caps and trainers? The cast wear doublets, hose and hats, and, later, plumed helmets and shining armour. One character jumps onto the stage, rests his can of lager on the ledge of one of the stage pillars, delivers his speech, and leaps back into the crowd of goundlings. The soothsayer barges through the ranks of the yard audience to exclaim "this street is narrow" before being given a leg-up onto the stage by nearby spectators in the yard, and when Cassius talks of a Caesar who "doth bestride the narrow world / Like a Colossus," the stage pillars complete the image visually.

A factor that has become more apparent with every season is the space's resistance to too much naturalism. Artifice, self-conscious and not, can be quite blatant on this stage. It does seem from early performances at the new Globe that representational effects may do little to aid the audience's imagination. And this could be because such devices are conspicuously re-presentational on an open playhouse stage under an unfocused, unforgiving light that offers neither the self-proclaimed deception of theatrical "magic realism" nor the carefully contrived naturalism that aims to pass itself off as "real life." The space seems to resist attempts to provide it with much "help" in turning it into a clearly delineated setting, whether it be a midsummer night in a wood outside Athens, a cold dawn on the vasty fields of France, the middle of the night in Brutus's orchard in ancient

Rome, the dead of night in a Scottish castle, or a freezing midnight on the battlements of a Danish castle.

I am beginning to question, again, whether illusionism was the norm at the original Globe. Of course the written evidence we have suggests there were different views on this question by commentators and practitioners at the time. In one description of Burbage's acting, as Richard III, a playgoer is said to have "mistook a player for a king./ For when he would have said, King Richard died, / And call'd—a horse! A horse! He, Burbage cried."[4] In another reference to Burbage, each role subsumes the actor: "No more young Hamlet, old Hieronymo, / King Lear, the grieved Moor," and when he "but seem'd to bleed" spectators in the audience and on the stage, "Amazed, thought even then he died indeed."[5] Ben Jonson's famously witty deriding of Shakespeare's cavalier attitude to the neo-classical unities is given added weight when you are standing in the new Globe's yard listening to Time slide over sixteen years and waft us from Sicily over the seas to Bohemia. Jonson, in the Folio version of one of his plays, printed five or six years after *The Winter's Tale* at the Globe, tells us that he won't be expecting his audience to believe that a nation at civil war can be represented by three rusty swords. Shakespeare seemed to relish fiction's power to compel belief by actually telling his audience that he has only "four or five most vile and ragged foils / Right ill-disposed in brawl ridiculous" to depict the mighty battle of Agincourt. Jonson eschews such illusionistic poverty. His plays will not

> purchase your delight at such a rate,
> As, for it, he himself must justly hate:
> To make a child, now swaddled, to proceed
> Man and then shoot up, in one beard and weed,
> Past three score years; or, with three rusty swords,
> And help of some few foot and half-foot words,
> Fight over York and Lancaster's long jars:
> And in the tiring-house bring wounds to scars.
> He rather prays, you will be pleas'd to see
> One such, today as other plays should be;
> Whether neither Chorus wafts you ore the seas;
> Nor creaking throne comes down, the boys to please;
> Nor nimble squibbe is seene, to make afear'd
> The Gentlewoman; nor roul'd bullet heard
> To say, it thunders; nor tempestuous drum

> Rumbles, to tell you when the storm has come.
> *Every Man In His Humour* 1616 Folio

Jonson's apparent frustration with the mimetic inadequacies of play-acting is given a fresh impetus by experiencing performances at the reconstruction of the theater where *Every Man In* was performed by the King's Men in 1605 (it was originally performed in 1598 by the Chamberlain's Men, probably at the Curtain theater with Shakespeare, Burbage, and Kemp in the cast). The theater conditions of an open playhouse offer a clearer understanding, I think, of the physical constraints of attempting verisimilitude in such a space, whether it is a sixteenth-century theater or a twentieth-century one.

Experiments with exits and entrances on the new Globe stage have begun, I think, to shed some significant light on how the plays *play* on such a large stage. Overlapping exits and entrances seem to be a necessary piece of staging. It takes two or three lines for an actor to move from an entry door in the *frons scenae*—the wall at the back of the stage—to the front of the stage. If the stage is empty, the energy levels drop, which must have something to do with the auditorium and stage being in the same light. In a darkened auditorium, the stage can go dark or have some kind of lighting directed on to it to provide a kind of continuity to the fiction. In a theater like the new Globe the audience is more likely to become part of the fiction, so that if the stage is at any time without actor or action the playgoers are momentarily without a role, in a way that they would not be in a proscenium arch theater, where there is usually a set or at least some props left on the stage platform.

The experiments on Bankside suggest that the two corners upstage are powerful positions. Actors found that the extreme edges outside the pillars were "hot" spots for interacting with the playgoers. Here, the actor is in touch with the audience in direct and tangible ways: The pillar has the effect of separating the corner spot from the rest of the stage. It is a natural place to deliver a soliloquy and other forms of direct address to the audience. Even when the actor has turned in to the stage to interact with other characters on the stage platform, the audience is "with" him or her. This is an important discovery for dramaturgical positioning on the stage; a character automatically has the audience on his or her "side," unless there is a compelling reason for the audience's hostility to the character. Even this qualification will need to be tested further: does the power of this position itself extend to encouraging audiences to empathize or become engaged with a character whose actions are morally reprehensible? What will happen when Richard Gloucester stands at the corner of the stage to let us in on his plans to murder his way to the throne? Or when Macbeth does the same? How much will the dramaturgical possibilities of the physical proximity of actor and playgoer in shared light contribute to the audience's sense of complicity?

The "authority" position on the stage is under the "fiery cloud" on the heavens trap, in the middle of the stage width, forward of the frons, and back from the pillars. It is this spot at which all the spectators' sightlines converge and thus offers the least obstruction from the stage pillars.

The physical effects on the physical experience of the actors in the space are what has struck me most from my researches on the first seasons. Definition in action required by an open thrust, flexible stage, free of the clutter of props and furniture, has a profound effect on character and structure, not least because the space fosters a relativist attitude to time and place. Flexibility is a key word here. Dramaturgical possibilities seem to be infinite, and if you are an effective playwright writing for such a space you would automatically use the physical features of your theater to their full potential. If you are offered a space which allows—even demands—relativity of time and place, you could not, as a dramatist, ignore the opportunities it provides when structuring your play and creating its characters, although Ben Jonson, with his constant striving for adherence to classical unities, for whom delineating time and location was a paramount concern, would probably not agree.

Notes

1. Platter, Thomas. 1959. *Travels in England, 1599.* Translated by Clare Williams. London: 1959.

2. For a valuable account of the design and construction of the new Globe, see Greenfield, Jon. 1997. "Design as Reconstruction: Reconstruction as Design," and "Timber Framing, the Two Bays and After." Both in *Shakespeare's Globe Rebuilt*, edited by J. R. Mulryne and Margaret Shewring. Cambridge: Cambridge University Press, 81–120. Greenfield is exemplary on the value of ranking source material.

3. See Orrell, John. 1997. "Designing the Globe: Reading the Documents." In Mulryne and Shewring 1997, 51–65.

4. *Iter Boreale* c. 1618, in Poems of Richard Corbet. Quoted in Salgado, Gamini, ed. 1975. *Eyewitnesses of Shakespeare*. Sussex: Harvester Press, 37–38.

5. *A Funeral Elegy on the Death of the Famous Actor Richard Burbage Who Died on Saturday* In *Lent the 13th* of March 1618. In Salgado 1975, 38–39.

Tracking Performance Criticism of Shakespeare

Marvin Rosenberg

In September 1939, *PMLA* published "Elizabethan Actors," then a rare essay of the kind we now call "performance criticism," which draws on the practice of the theater to illuminate dramatic work.

The *PMLA* essay was by Alfred Harbage, whose books had earned the immense respect of Shakespeare seventeenth-century drama scholars. He was synthesizing an orthodox academic attitude toward the function of acting in the Elizabethan theater. His word carried great weight. For at least a dozen years no significant scholarly voice would be raised in disagreement. And Harbage was very wrong.

His essay provided a good lesson for performance critics to come. He argued from a learned deduction: presumably Shakespearean—Elizabethan—acting was quite different in kind from what we know today. Harbage voiced a familiar concept among many Renaissance scholars that the Shakespearean theater was committed to language, the words were everything: the actors were depersonalized mouthpieces who recited the dramatic poetry without allowing any individuality of characterization to distract from the verbal drama. Given this basic axiom, unreal deductions had to follow. Stage business must have been minimized, action formalized. The acting was not "natural," but a system of gestural patterns, as in oratory. Women's roles were acted by males, *argal* nonnaturally.

The weighty authority of Harbage and other distinguished scholars ("formalists") pointed logically to an image of actors as puppets who almost mechanically gave voice to the playwright's words. And the image was widely accepted.

With the persistence of this misconception, any effective critical approach to Shakespeare's *playwriting* art was hardly possible. His *dramatic* art was being submitted to analytic method for literary forms encountered only on the page. When B. L. Joseph reasserted the formalist conception eleven years after Harbage, in 1951 (*Elizabethan Acting*), he put its uselessness for performance criticism squarely:

> In the theater, as in the study, the poet's words are all that count. . . . We must be prepared to respond to Elizabethan drama *in the same attitude of mind as we respond to opera or ballet before we can hope to criticize the dramatist's techniques justly*. (Joseph 1951, italics mine)

Joseph here articulated the formalist failure to consider the organism of dramatic art. Trapped in the perspective that equated the experience from the stage with that in the armchair, Joseph neglected the special, variable art of the actor, and took refuge again in the monopoly of language:

> given two actors of equal talent, each would be able to perform the same speech in exactly the same way, apart from differences of voice and personal appearance. (Joseph 1951,)

Any formalist could have known better by simply consulting either or both of the two beacons that shed light on performance practice. One is the sense of the dramatic art itself, of which more in a moment. The second, more practical, intellectually accessible, involves a familiar scholarly strategy: a study of the relevant printed materials—the records that tell what actually happened in the theater, as found in playscripts, official documents, biographies, memoirs, gossip, social and political debates, promptbooks, fugitive remarks—(and later, formal reviews)—"performance history." There was more than enough of it even in the scanty sixteenth and seventeenth-century record to demonstrate that the playwrights were mainly aiming at a lifelike, poetically natural "realism," of the sort Shakespeare intended in the *Henry VIII* prologue:

> Think ye see
> The very persons of our noble story
> As they were living.
> (Prologue, 25–27)

The first searchlight on drama as performance, mentioned above, imaginative participation in the artistic activity itself, is necessarily more personal. It asks a sympathy with actors and the context in which they move, a readiness to share vicariously in the physical and spiritual possibilities of their art and in the objectives of their characters, whose portrayal moves audiences to laughter, thought, and tears. This is the next closest thing to knowing the art of drama by physically participating in it.

Every critic knows that Shakespeare's lines are not only made up of words, but also of passions. If a formalist had only practiced reading, as if acting it, the text of one of the great characters, he/she would surely have felt how, individually for him/her, the sounded, felt words plucked at feelings and muscles, how body and passion could be jerked into the desperate or joyful activity that audiences would instantly recognize, in its many variations, as "natural" badges of all our tribe.

Often the imagined action would have had to include some presumed prop in hand to energize movement, for Shakespeare keeps providing *things* which force characters to interaction—gifts, letters, miscellaneous papers, furniture, ropes, chains, food, lanterns, items of clothing, weapons, etc. These familiar objects again and again enhance the "naturalness" of Shakespeare's actions. The formalists could only have deduced that Elizabethan acting was nonnatural because they had not experienced the performance activity.

What happened to me now becomes part of the story, as Enobarbus would say, of how performance criticism has contributed—and how it can—to our experience of Shakespeare's art. I was starting out in the 1950s collecting reminders from the Shakespearean period of the "naturalism" of Renaissance plays and their actors, and corollary evidences of the effect of natural acting on the emotions of audiences. These organized themselves into a paper countering the formalists. I offered it to the Shakespeare section of the annual MLA meeting in Boston in 1952. I could cite Elizabethan-Jacobean spectators moved to tears by the lifelikeness of the acting; demonstrations that males who acted women were no more "artificial" than are similar actors who seem wholly "natural" today; evidence that creative actors did not express themselves in fixed patterns because some orators' manuals urged physical clichés on speakers. I could note how hack actors were criticized within the playtexts—as by Buckingham in *Richard III*—for stereotyping gestures; by contrast the truly talented were glorified—like one who was praised for "so wholly transforming himself in his Part, and putting off himself with his Cloathes, as he never (not so much as in the Tyring-house), assum'd himself again until the play was done." (Heywood 1622,) The ideal was a recognizably "natural" image of the characterization intended: "a souldier, shap'd like a souldier, walke, speake, act like a souldier." How could the spectators not be moved?

> What English blood seeing the person of any bold English man presented and doth not hugge his fame ... As if the Personator were the man Personated, so bewitching a thing is lively and spirited action.
>
> (Heywood 1622,)

My point: the performance record, and a sense of participation in the dramatic art form, could surely have been called on to demonstrate that there was no single, monolithic Elizabethan variety of acting, as there was none in the dramatic varieties of tragedy, comedy, slapstick, fantasy, pastoral, maybe even masque. Except where action might be intentionally antinatural, the playwrights wanted to capture a recognizable experience of human life in action. And actors, as always, wanted in their individual ways to move audiences.

What happened to my paper should be heartening to any scholar, and it left me with enormous new respect for Harbage. I was encouraged to submit my piece to *PMLA*, and it was sent to Harbage as one of the readers. He could easily have brushed it aside; but his comment, which he allowed to be sent me, said simply that he did not agree with me, but he felt my point of view had a right to be heard, so he recommended it for publication ("Elizabethan Actors: Men or Marionettes," September 1954, reprinted in *The Seventeenth Century Theater*). My admiration for Harbage was further increased when he later, in a *Shakespeare Quarterly* review, acknowledged—as would Joseph, ultimately—that the formalist concept was inadequate. May we all be as flexible, as generous and as honest.

Since Shakespeare offers—besides all the delightful attractions of his texts—the best opportunity for a scholar interested in exploring the contribution of the theatrical dimension, I thereafter mainly worked with his drama. My experience may help to illuminate the development of performance criticism.

I found at midcentury this approach was a lonely endeavor. With one valuable exception, noted below, academic scholars for many years had learned to study Shakespeare primarily as a poet. They were—are—doing admirable work in mining and appreciating his language and imagery, and in exploring his historical and cultural context. We all owe them a great debt. Actors and directors have been particularly grateful for the scholarly discoveries that gave meaning to words that had become obscure or ambiguous.

But when these scholars dealt with Shakespeare's characterization, it was often in a kind of vacuum: they avoided testing their hypotheses in the conditions of theater in which Shakespeare has practiced his art. Academicians could hardly be blamed for keeping the stage at arm's length, as their mentors also had. The theater had long carried a touch of the raffish about it; in some cultures actors had not been regarded as first-class citizens, could not even be buried with their respectable fellows. And for as long as anybody knew, the commercial stage had committed such crimes against Shakespeare's texts and characters that serious admirers might understandably prefer to avoid it, as sensitive men like Lamb did. *Lear* had been unrecognizable for a century and a half; even *Hamlet* could be wrecked, as Garrick demonstrated, unforgivably.

In the eighteenth and nineteenth centuries, texts had been amputated to make room for greedy stage machinery and the popular afterpieces. The forces of purity were shamefully censoring Shakespeare's language, substituting lily-whitened words for the hearty originals so important to character and theme, or cutting out chunks entirely. As late as the 1950s, the word *whore* could not be spoken in an *Othello* staging.

Little wonder that scholars, not comfortable with Shakespeare's theater profession, were slow to embrace this part of his art. The great Bradley, for instance, seemed embarrassed in his few allusions to it. In fact he himself occasionally tried to imagine the characters in interaction; but he could not easily accept the texts' implied, subverbal stage activity. Typically, in a rare allusion to the theater, he rejected Bernhardt's (as Lady Macbeth) subtle, seductive persuasion of Macbeth to murder. This was regarded by many spectators as an artistic achievement and often since imitated. Bradley, fixed on the conventional Sara Siddons image of Lady Macbeth as evil, could not yield to Bernhardt's intuition; he could find no specific words to justify her physical language.

Because Bradley wanted to think of the mad Ophelia as always "sweet and lovable," he wrote that in Ophelia's "wanderings we hear from time to time an undertone of deepest sorrow, but never the agonized cry of fear or horror which makes madness dreadful or shocking." And in a footnote:

> I have heard an actress in this part utter such a cry as is described above, but there is absolutely nothing in the text to justify her rendering.

But actresses often hear, in Ophelia's words, and Shakespeare's description of her troubled activity ("nods, becks . . . Spurns . . . beats her heart"), a subtext of strenuous signs of madness. Bradley's ear was not tuned to the unspoken contributions Shakespeare expected from actors, and he made no critical effort to discover the theater's illuminations that enrich the historical staging record.

Fortunately, that record was expanding. Rich stores of information on the theaters' contributions to Shakespeare's meanings would become available, as journalism on the drama flourished throughout Europe. The stage would always be a fascinating subject, and writers began to build a treasure house on how Shakespeare was being acted. There were true performance critics, like Hazlitt evaluating Kean, and using him to explore the Shakespearean plays he acted in. There were many lesser writers, performance historians at least, who faithfully saw all the Shakespeare they could, compared actors and characterizations and theatrical techniques, carried us through changes in lighting and scenography, lobbied for improvements in acting style and return to the first texts.

Some writers piled up rich portraits-in-depth of particular actors, sometimes in specific roles. Distinguished performers from throughout Europe, England, America, and Asia, became the subject of books and articles which detailed their great characterizations. The actors themselves generally avoided verbalizing their artistic intuitions, but a few have left records of their art, in autobiography or interview.

So much attention began to be paid to theater and its personalities that great libraries and national and international theater institutes would form, to collect documents, books, newspaper reviews, and the burgeoning irregular data that becomes available. Private notebooks, scrapbooks, and random clippings would go into the files. Increasingly performance historians would be able to cite *anon* and *unidentified* for bits recovered from miscellaneous collections, which are worth poring through if only for the buried report of a single actor's gesture that may light up a whole corner of a characterization.

The sheer rising bulk of data required that performance history become a recognized discipline. The very existence of the great depositories invited scholars to visit them. Society got past its ambiguous attitude to the theater, and could allow actors generally to associate on even terms with gentlefolk, attend universities, and even be buried in "hallowed" ground. The stage—its structures, its facilities, its evolution, even its people—became a respectable area of study.

In academe, the one startling exception before 1950 to the study of Shakespeare only as text pointed the way, for any who noticed, to performance criticism. This was Arthur Colby Sprague's *Shakespeare and the Actors* (1944). Sprague collected, from wherever he could find them, records of stage business in Shakespeare's plays. Others had done this as supplementary bits and pieces; Sprague demonstrated that it was a study in itself. This was performance history and more. Sprague recognized that the language of Shakespeare's gestures could be as much a part of his artistic genius as the gestures of his language.

Scholars who really read Sprague could be prompted to see how a single illuminating piece of stage business could be meaningful and worth recording even if the production's remaining mutilated text was beneath contempt; how theater images sometimes worked against verbal surfaces; how silences could speak loudly; how actors could convey different shades of their characters' passions: love, madness, age, triumph. Now critics who allowed Shakespeare any dramatic art could learn a new skill: to explore more deeply the verbal, aesthetic and social values of the great texts by relating them to visual and aural dimensions that could illuminate them. Performance criticism was coming of age.

It took awhile for some to regard Shakespeare whole as a playwright-poet, but those who took the plunge into the exciting context of the theater in the last half-century could discover new depths and perspectives in the artworks. The process continues, the exploration ever deepening.

Now performance critics, often drawing on the resources of both literary scholarship and theatrical disciplines, help us to evaluate Shakespeare's art in the form in which he created it. When Alan Dessen, for instance, comments on a production he describes in detail, we are almost as good as at the Globe; we can turn to scholars like Herbert Coursen for perspectives on patterns of staging over the years.

We learn from examining the visual roots of the text, and the subtextual undercurrents, how a simple moment of action sometimes confers poetry on words that would be bare without it. There is, for instance, nothing inherently poetic in Ophelia saying

> There, my lord.

as she offers to return Hamlet's remembrances. But the words as spoken sound a deeply poetic physical-psychic moment, of emotions compressed and whipsawed, precious treasure sacrificed, dreams of a lifetime trembling in the balance. Not accidentally does the delicate crisis in the man-woman relationship fascinate audiences. At stake is the eternal mystery of inward human torment, and of the love between men and women, and of our dreams of union between them.

The performance critic studies the motivation for this gift-return of Ophelia's, and how her gestures might manifest interiority. Her own impulse? Showing hurt because Hamlet did not breach the wall she put around her? To provoke Hamlet to a reassertion of love? Her mind already close to breaking? How much Polonius' idea? What does she *do, feel* that helps reveal Shakespeare's art in depth of characterization? How have actors done it?

The critic who goes to research resources or to editors sensitive to the theatrical dimension, like Jay Halio, finds that Ophelias have manifested in various ways the almost intolerable pressure of conflicting feelings in those simplest of three words. Thus, she has thrown down the gifts, and the rich words accompanying them—the things and letters and poems so loaded with memories. Has tried to force them into Hamlet's hands. Has held them close even as she reluctantly offers them. Has whispered. Wept. Spoken loudly to be sure to be heard behind the arras. And she will go on finding new ways.

Another challenge here. Can the critic remember the first exposure to *Hamlet*? To evaluate Shakespeare's gift for building expectation, I have shown *Hamlet* (and other plays I've studied) to "naive spectators" who have never read or seen the play, or known its story, to recover fresh first responses. Universally for *Hamlet* one of the dominant hopes and expectations is for a happy ending together for Hamlet and Ophelia—right up to the shock of Gertrude's report of the death. We who already know Ophelia is dead, and will not forget it, must somehow willingly suspend memory to experience the playwright's initial creative strategy.

One enormously liberating effect on scholars who pay attention to performance history has been the realization that criticism can no longer pin the great characters down to single interpretations. The stage demonstrated, for those who studied it, that there could be many Lears, or Macbeths, or Hamlets, all following the text, but finding different emphases in the lines and direction. This had always been common knowledge among actors: creative artists, they had the impulse to originality common to their genius, and they expected it in others. Scholars had also sought original interpretations, but they worked in a tradition that prized a definitive, exclusive image for a character: *the* Hamlet, *the* Lear, *the* Othello.

Even Granville-Barker, a most highly intelligent theater man, sought to enclose characters in his descriptions; but there was not room in them for all the possible, meaningful characterizations the texts contained. Fortunately an eloquent scholar-director like John Russell Brown comes along to teach us better, broaden our perspectives.

The performance critic, who finds so many shades of personality in a Shakespeare character, may sometimes wonder: is there no core identity to explore? Yes; but only in discovering its varieties in the participatory nature of the art form, that accommodates so many different actors' interpretations. The metaphor I have used for the matching of the actor with the character is *polyphony*. Shakespeare's great characters are composed—as we are—of multiple, tremendously complex human qualities (or tones)—sometimes quite contradictory, as in Hamlet: e.g. kind and cruel, loving and savage (even murderous), fearful and fearless, masterful and submissive, sometimes both opposites at the same time, sometimes struggling between them. At any one moment, the changing combinations of tones—the polyphonies—determine the personalities we—or our characters—project.

Shakespeare evidently could count on his actors to find in a character those qualities best suited to their own qualities and their capacities for expression. Changing cultural contexts, and theatrical objectives, as well as personal inclination, would affect character emphases. Forbes Robertson, at the turn of the twentieth century, heard and sounded, in the Hamlet character tones, the notes of a kind, sweet gentleman-Hamlet who could hardly say a harsh word, who allowed himself violence only when forced. This polyphony commonly gave way, near the mid-twentieth century, to darker notes in aggressive Hamlets who heard more readily the toughness and cruelty in the character. In a backlash, Hamlet has sometimes become again a more lovable prince. Ideally, as many of the tones as possible will resonate.

The performance critic set free to enter each character in an adventure among depths learns to let artistic intuition share guidance with knowledge and literary training. Thus: what are the suggestions from performance history? From literary theorists? How do they match one's own polyphony? When I worked on *Othello*, I asked Laurence Olivier what he thought of Ernest Jones's suggestion that Iago's fierce hostility to Othello masked a repressed homosexual impulse. Olivier had hinted this conception in his acting of Iago, some years before; now it was "not one to which I would any longer subscribe." He saw Iago as a mass of complexes; and as for homosexuality, "as it exists entirely in the subconscious, there is no object in touching on it in any details of performance."

I come back into the story. When I directed the tragedy, and played Iago, I did not subscribe to the theory either; but as a performance critic I had the luxury of probing into my polyphony, and asking why my bitter self could seem to love no one, except ostensibly Desdemona in private. Why did Shakespeare design (my) Iago's tremendous concentration on Othello? Why the accompanying frustration which gave him such sheer physical pain? —

> doth like a poisonous mineral
> Gnaw my inwards.
> (2.1.198)

Many tones could be felt to fuse in the cramps Iago—and I as Iago—felt; what sounded was the mystery of human personality. In some such way the performance critic can probe—even analyze—himself as the character he undertakes; he can run through the tones in the polyphony of both and discover which sound truest, and ask why.

Acting—or fully imagining—a role can be the performance critic's balancing to theory. Wilson Knight learned this with *Othello*. Knight had a soaring imagination, and liked to comprehend Shakespeare's dramas in symbolic terms. He sought a key to make *Othello* "yield to a mating with his mind" (a curious image, I thought, that seems to whisper "assault.") What Knight settled on was the image of Iago as "undefined, devisualized, inhuman. . . . Once this is clear, the whole play begins to have meaning."

Then Knight had the brave idea to produce the play; and after it the sense to realize that his symbolism was disastrous "if allowed to interfere with the expressly domestic and human qualities of the drama." He found that Shakespeare had written a play about people.

I earnestly believe in scholars acting out scenes and whole plays for themselves and with their students and associates to illuminate moments of character and action. I have learned a good deal from it. Few of us are blessed with enough acting talent to portray professionally Shakespeare's characters, but there is still comfort: striking perceptions may result from an earnest critic's solo recreations. Not trying to *act* the characters, but to *be* them—to share their identities. No need—as the actor has—to worry about the presence of an audience. Rather to assemble interiorly Shakespeare's multiple polyphonic clues to human nature into a poetic characterization, be

> The very persons of our noble story
> As they were living.
> (*Henry VIII*, Prologue, 26)

Me again. I do try privately in the study to sense what the actors search for: the felt life, the subtexts, of the characters they personate—first reading aloud the lines, sometimes recording them. I find a kind of triple awareness operating. I say the words for their denotations and connotations—and here I always find myself silently thanking the philologists for rescuing meanings that are lost, confused, or obsolete.

Meanwhile, I am listening to the sounds, for puns, for music, for silences, for the emotions and interactions that signal character in gestation. And I find the very saying of the words evokes character dimensions that spring to life within me: my body alerts me to kinesthetic responses that Shakespeare surely meant to accompany and often accent the language.

In my study I have played some instructive roles. Thus, when I was privately experiencing *Measure for Measure*, I was in her turn attracted to the character of Isabella. (For a performance critic, gender is no barrier; men exult imaginatively in women's roles, women in men's.) As I sensed the carriage, the gestures, the clothes, the accents of this high-spirited, sexually repressed girl, who began as a novice (and might be so dressed) wanting even more restrictions than the convent imposed; so sure of her virginal morality that she would not for a moment consider yielding it even to save her own brother's life; turning so daring and stern and fiery against Angelo, the highest power in the land—how would I-Isabella react when at the end I was ridiculed before the whole populace as a mad and lying nun, and made to believe my brother had been executed—all lies by a fake monk who turned out to be a practical-joker-Duke who then asked me to marry him?

In all the stagings I had seen, Isabella tamely agreed to the marriage; but I felt such a submission would die on my lips. Proud and passionate as I was, would I conceivably agree to *marry* the man? Though he asks twice, Shakespeare does not give Isabella lines to accept, nor could I imagine doing it as the character, I felt Shakespeare surely intended rejection, so that this Duke of dark corners is checked in his curious hubris, and Isabella can go on untouched by the climate of discolored marriages scheduled around her. I urged such rejection in a paper to the International Shakespeare Association conference at Stratford; two years later the *Measure for Measure* staging there by the Royal Shakespeare Company used my ending—the first time known in the theater, Ralph Berry reported in one of his fine studies—but employed by various theaters since. We must be open to our polyphonies—mine evidently matched that of some Isabellas, and of some minds.

Any scholar could be helped to experience imaginatively a complex character, as I was, by various actors' routines for inhabiting their roles. I will mention two.

Stanislavsky (I will simplify here) proposed a double approach. The actor could work from the outside, imagining or actually wearing the character's clothes: before he himself played Othello, Stanislavsky went about his daily life in the Moor's robe. Stanislavsky did not later have so much faith in this technique; but I have found that clothes, real or imaginary, can impress identity on me: when I felt, in the imagined novice garment that I chose for Isabella, the weight, the formality, and the austerity, it conditioned my character intuitions. I have found the principle useful for other personae.

To absorb a character's *interior*, Stanislavsky proposed emotional memory: for Isabella's indignation with Angelo, the actor could draw on the energy from a moment of arousal revived in imagination from his/her own past.

Performance critics can also join with actors—and directors—in looking for a "key" or metaphor for a character in a play, or a scene. Thus, for Ophelia's mad scene: Tyrone Guthrie suggested to one of his Ophelias a wild animal clawing. A colleague of mine, Martin Berman, proposed that the actresses in his workshop imagine themselves walking a very high, very narrow ridge. This matched, interestingly, the German critic Tieck's nineteenth-century image: "We are made prophetically to see upon what a dizzy height her whole being totters." A kinesthetic activity is sometimes encouraged: Gielgud told one of his Ophelias to go to her dressing room and frighten herself to death. Berman suggested that Ophelia might, before entering, spin round and come in a touch dizzy.

I'm sure performance criticism burgeons when it can draw on both a scholar's familiarity with the document under study and the voicing of an imagined experience of its staging. For help in speaking the text, see Patsy Rodenburg's *The Need for Words*.

The text is bedrock, read and reinforced in observation or performance if possible. I always attend rehearsals and final stagings of a play when I set out to do a book or essay. With Shakespeare I never tire of the words; and sometimes the heard repetitions enforce a perception of special structures. So for my *Lear* study my ear told me after several rehearsals how very important *if* was in consonance with the tensions of the physical imagery, and how, with other small words of measure and difference, it affected the whole visual-verbal balance of the play.

We cannot always attend performances, and the plays we are studying seem often fatefully to be staged far off; but technology is beginning to enable us to see some of them anyway. For my *Hamlet* book I managed to study—besides the available films—forty videotapes of performances sent me from all the Scandinavian countries, from most of Eastern and Western Europe, England, Canada, America, Israel, and Japan. (Alas, it is not always so easy: not nearly as many tapes are available for *Antony and Cleopatra*, the play I am now studying.)

The tapes are not the same thing as live performance, but can still be highly rewarding. Like any good stagings, they can introduce us to actors' new visualizations of Shakespeare's lines that make us perceive them as for the first time, and encourage us to imagine new actions on our own.

This is the special value of performance criticism to Shakespeareans—that we will get to know the plays more intimately, interiorly, in their live dimension for which Shakespeare created them, as well as in their literary and historic identities. So will our students, who are being better prepared by the growth of dramatic study in the schools.

That we who learn to appreciate Shakespeare's gifts as a playwright-poet are personally and professionally enriched is manifested in the work of a whole generation of Shakespeareans who have brought the theater into their writing in the last half-century. The discipline of performance criticism has brought forth such fine collections of essays as Marvin and Ruth Thompson's *Shakespeare and the*

Sense of Performance, and thoughtful, thought-provoking volumes like John Styan's *The Shakespeare Revolution,* William Worthen's *Shakespeare and the Authority of Performance,* James Bulman's *Shakespeare, Theory and Performance,* and Michael Goldman's books and essays.

If not all of our colleagues will want to participate in performance criticism, how much there is for them still to discover in the traditional areas of study: about the language of the texts, the Elizabethan-Jacobean culture and history, the relevances of psychology, the life of the artist. We can all be grateful for the resulting insights. Meanwhile, I believe those of us who do also draw Shakespeare's theater art into our study, experience it, plumb its depths, and channel it into our teaching, may enrich our students, our colleagues, our lives.

Bibliography

Adams, John Cranford. 1961. *The Globe Playhouse.* New York: Barnes & Noble.

Alexander, Bill. 1989. Interview in *On Directing Shakespeare: Interviews with Contemporary Directors,* by Ralph Berry. London: Hamish Hamilton.

Ball, Robert Hamilton. 1968. *Shakespeare on Silent Film.* London: George Allen & Unwin.

Bartholomeusz, Dennis. 1969. *Macbeth and the Players.* Cambridge: Cambridge University Press.

Barton, John. 1984. *Playing Shakespeare.* London: Methuen.

Basinger, Jeanine. 1999. *Silent Stars.* New York: Knopf.

Bate, Jonathan, and Russell Jackson. 1996. *Shakespeare: An Illustrated Stage History.* Oxford: Oxford University Press.

Beckerman, Bernard. 1962. *Shakespeare at the Globe, 1599–1609.* New York: Macmillan.

Berry, Ralph. 1993. *Shakespeare in Performance: Castings and Metamorphoses.* London: Macmillan.

Bradbrook, Muriel. 1932. *Elizabethan Stage Conditions: A Study of Their Place in the Interpretation of Shakespeare's Plays.* Cambridge: Cambridge University Press.

Bradley, A. C. 1904. *Shakespearean Tragedy.* London: Macmillan.

Brockbank, Philip, ed. 1985. *Players of Shakespeare 1.* Cambridge: Cambridge University Press.

Brown, John Russell, ed. 1982. *Focus on "Macbeth."* London: Routledge and Kegan Paul.

———. 1993. *Shakespeare's Plays in Performance.* New York: Applause.

———. 1996. *William Shakespeare: Writing for Performance.* New York: St. Martin's.

Brubach, Holly. 1999. *Girlfriend: Men, Women, and Drag.* New York: Random House.

Bulman, James, ed. 1996. *Shakespeare, Theory, and Performance.* London: Routledge.

Cohen, Robert. 1991. *Acting in Shakespeare.* London: Mayfield.

Coursen, Herbert. 1995. *Reading Shakespeare on Stage.* Newark: University of Delaware Press.

———. 1997. *Teaching Shakespeare with Film and TV.* Westport, CT: Greenwood.

Coursen, Herbert, and James Bulman, eds. 1988. *Shakespeare on Television.* Hanover, NH: University Press of New England.

David, Richard. 1978. *Shakespeare in the Theater.* Cambridge: Cambridge University Press.

Dessen, Alan. 1977. *Elizabethan Drama and the Viewer's Eye.* Chapel Hill: University of North Carolina Press.

———. 1984. *Elizabethan Stage Conventions and Modern Interpreters*. Cambridge: Cambridge University Press.

———. 1995. *Recovering Shakespeare's Theatrical Vocabulary*. Cambridge: Cambridge University Press.

Doran, Gregory. 1993. "Solanio in *The Merchant of Venice*." In *Players of Shakespeare 3*, edited by Russell Jackson and Robert Smallwood. Cambridge: Cambridge University Press.

Elam, Keir. 1996. "In What Chapter of His Bosom?" In *Alternative Shakespeares 2*, edited by Terrence Hawkes. London: Routledge.

Ellis-Fermor, Una. 1961. *Shakespeare the Dramatist*. Edited by Kenneth Muir. London: Methuen.

Evans, Gareth Lloyd. 1982. "*Macbeth*: 1946–80 at Stratford-upon-Avon." In Brown, *Focus on "Macbeth."*

Foakes, R. A., ed. 1968. *Macbeth*. New York: Bobbs-Merrill.

———. 1982. "Images of death: ambition in *Macbeth*." In *Focus on "Macbeth,"* ed. J.R. Brown, 7–29.

Goldman, Michael. 1985. *Acting and Actions in Shakespearean Tragedy*. Princeton: Princeton University Press.

Granville-Barker, Harley. 1947. *Prefaces to Shakespeare*. 2 volumes. Princeton: Princeton University Press.

———. 1974. *More Prefaces to Shakespeare*. Princeton: Princeton University Press.

Gross, John. 1992. *Shylock*. London: Chatto & Windus.

Gurr, Andrew. 1970. *The Shakespearean Stage, 1574–1642*. Cambridge: Cambridge University Press.

———. 1996. *The Shakespearean Playing Companies*. Oxford: Oxford University Press.

Halio, Jay L. 1988. *Understanding Shakespeare's Plays in Performance*. Manchester: Manchester University Press.

Harbage, Alfred. 1939. "Elizabethan Actors." *PMLA* 54, 685–708.

———. 1941. *Shakespeare's Audience*. New York: Columbia University Press.

Hattaway, Michael. 1982. *Elizabethan Popular Theater: Plays in Performance*. London.

Hinman, Charlton, ed. 1968. *The First Folio of Shakespeare*. New York: W. W. Norton.

Hodges, C. Walter. 1968. *The Globe Restored*. New York: Coward-McCann.

Holden, Stephen. 1996. "There's Something Verboten in Illyria." *New York Times*, 25 October, C3.

Holland, Peter. 1997. *English Shakespeare: Shakespeare on The English Stage in the 1990s*. Cambridge: Cambridge University Press.

Hosley, Richard. 1964. "The Origins of the Shakespearean Playhouse." *Shakespeare Quarterly* 15:29–39.

Jackson, Russell, and Robert Smallwood, eds. 1988. *Players of Shakespeare 2*. Cambridge: Cambridge University Press.

Joseph, Bertram. 1964. *Elizabethan Acting*. Second, revised edition. Oxford: Oxford University Press.

Kennedy, Dennis. 1993. *Looking at Shakespeare: A Visual History of Twentieth Century Performance.* Cambridge: Cambridge University Press.

Kiernan, Pauline. 1999. *Staging Shakespeare at the New Globe.* London: Macmillan.

King, Thomas. 1971. *Shakespearean Staging, 1599–1642.* Cambridge: Harvard University Press.

Kliman, Bernice W. 1992. *Shakespeare in Performance: Macbeth.* Manchester: Manchester University Press.

Knight, G. Wilson. 1949. *The Wheel of Fire.* London: Methuen.

Lusardi, James P. 1992. "Shakespeare's Performed Words, *Macbeth* and Improvisation in the Classroom." *CEA Critic* 54.2 (Winter): 21–29.

Lusardi, James P., and June Schlueter. 1991. *Reading Shakespeare in Performance: "King Lear."* Madison, NJ: Fairleigh Dickinson University Press.

Luscombe, Christopher. 1998. "Launcelot Gobbo in *The Merchant of Venice* and Moth in *Love's Labour's Lost.*" In *Players of Shakespeare 4*, edited by Robert Smallwood. Cambridge: Cambridge University Press.

Marks, Peter. 1996. "So Young, So Fragile, So Vexed about Sex." *New York Times.* 20 October, H13, H18.

Marrapodi, Michele, et al. 1993. *Shakespeare's Italy: Functions of Italian Locations in Renaissance Drama.* Manchester: Manchester University Press.

McCarthy, Mary. 1972. *The Stones of Florence and Venice Observed.* Harmondsworth: Penguin.

McDiarmid, Hugh. 1988. "Shylock in *The Merchant of Venice.*" In Jackson and Smallwood, *Players of Shakespeare 2.*

Miller, Jonathan. 1986. *Subsequent Performances.* London: Faber & Faber.

Muir, Kenneth. 1964. *Shakespeare's "Hamlet."* London: Arnold.

Mulryne, J. R., and Margaret Shewring, eds. 1997. *Shakespeare's Globe Rebuilt.* Cambridge: Cambridge University Press.

Neill, Heather. 1992. "Shylock's Pounded Flesh." *The Times*, 9 December.

Odell, G. C. D. 1966. *Shakespeare from Betterton to Irving.* 2 volumes. New York: Dover.

Orrell, John. 1982. *The Quest for Shakespeare's Globe.* Cambridge: Cambridge University Press.

Ripley, John. 1990. *"Julius Caesar" on Stage in England and America, 1599–1973.* Cambridge: Cambridge University Press.

Rosenberg, Marvin. 1961. *The Masks of Othello.* Berkeley: University of California Press.

———. 1972. *The Masks of King Lear.* Berkeley: University of California Press.

———. 1978. *The Masks of Macbeth.* Berkeley: University of California Press.

———. 1982. "Macbeth and Lady Macbeth in the Eighteenth and Nineteenth Centuries." In Brown, *Focus on "Macbeth."*

———. 1992. *The Masks of Hamlet.* Newark: University of Delaware Press.

——— 1997. *The Adventures of a Shakespeare Scholar.* Newark: University of Delaware Press.

Rothwell, Kenneth, and Annabelle Henken Melzer. 1990. *Shakespeare on Screen: An International Filmography and Videography.* New York: Neal-Schuman.

Rutter, Carol, et al. 1989. *Clamourous Voices: Shakespeare's Women Today.* New York: Routledge.

Smith, Irwin. 1964. *Shakespeare's Blackfriars Playhouse.* New York: New York University Press.

Speaight, Robert. 1973. *Shakespeare on Stage.* Boston: Little Brown.

Sprague, A. C. 1963. *Shakespeare and the Actors.* New York: Russell and Russell.

Stewart, Patrick. 1985. "Shylock." In *Players of Shakespeare 1,* edited by Philip Brockbank. Cambridge: Cambridge University Press.

Sturgess, Keith. 1987. *Jacobean Private Theater.* London: Routledge.

Styan, J. L. 1977. *The Shakespeare Revolution: Criticism and Performance in the Twentieth Century.* Cambridge: Cambridge Univ. Press.

Thomson, Peter. 1992. *Shakespeare's Theater.* Second edition. London: Routledge.

Thompson, Marvin and Ruth. 1989. *Shakespeare and the Sense of Performance.* Newark: University of Delaware Press.

Trewin, J. C. 1964. *Shakespeare on the English Stage, 1900–1964.* London: Barrie and Rockliff.

Tynan, Kenneth. 1994. *Letters.* Edited by Kathleen Tynan. London: Weidenfeld and Nicolson.

Wells, Stanley. 1977. *Royal Shakespeare: Four Major Productions at Stratford-upon-Avon.* Manchester: Manchester University Press.

Williams, Gary Jay. 1997. *Our Moonlight Revels: A Midsummer Night's Dream in the Theater.* Iowa City: University of Iowa Press.

Worthen, William. 1997. *Shakespeare and the Authority of Performance.* Cambridge: Cambridge University Press.

Wright, William. 1998. *Born That Way: Genes, Behavior, Personality.* New York: Knopf.

List of Contributors

RALPH BERRY has taught Shakespeare in universities throughout the world. Among his many books are *Shakespeare in Performance: Castings and Metamorphoses, Changing Styles in Shakespeare*, and *Shakespeare's Comedies: Explorations in Form*. He is currently a resident of Stratford-Upon-Avon.

JOHN RUSSELL BROWN has written many books, including *Shakespeare's Plays in Performance, Free Shakespeare, Shakespeare and His Comedies*, and most recently, *William Shakespeare: Writing for Performance* and *New Sites for Shakespeare*. He has edited Shakespeare, Webster, and *The Oxford Illustrated History of Theater*.

JAMES C. BULMAN is Professor of English at Allegheny College, where he has also been dean. He has also served recently as president of the Shakespeare Association of America. He is the general editor of Manchester's "Shakespeare in Performance" series and has recently edited *Shakespeare, Theory, and Performance*.

H. R. COURSEN has taught Shakespeare at many colleges and universities, and conducted workshops at various theaters and Shakespeare institutes. Among his twelve books on Shakespeare are *Christian Ritual in Shakespeare's Tragedies, Reading Shakespeare on Stage*, and with James Bulman, *Shakespeare on Television*. He is founder and coeditor of *Shakespeare and the Classroom*.

ALAN C. DESSEN is Peter G. Phialas Professor of English at the University of North Carolina, Chapel Hill, as well as performance editor of *Shakespeare Quarterly*. Among his several books on Shakespeare and Elizabethan drama are *Shakespeare and the Late Moral Plays, Recovering Shakespeare's Theatrical Vocabulary*, and the forthcoming *Dictionary of Stage Directions in English Drama, 1580–1642*. He is also the director of ACTER.

JAY L. HALIO is Professor of English at the University of Delaware; he is also a member of the editorial board of the University of

Delaware Press. He is the author or editor of more than twenty books on Shakespeare or contemporary fiction, among which are *Understanding Shakespeare's Plays in Performance* and editions of *Macbeth, The Merchant of Venice,* and *King Lear.*

HARRY KEYISHIAN is Professor of English at Fairleigh Dickinson University, where he is also editor of *The Literary Review* and director of the Fairleigh Dickinson University Press. Among his publications on Shakespeare is his *Shakespeare and the Shapes of Revenge.* He also conducts an annual Shakespeare colloquium at FDU.

PAULINE KIERNAN has been Research Fellow at the University of Reading and Leverhulme Research Fellow at the New Globe. She is the author of *Shakespeare's Theory of Drama* and *Staging Shakespeare at the New Globe.* She is also a prize-winning playwright.

JAMES P. LUSARDI is Francis A. March Professor of English at Lafayette College and coeditor with June Schlueter of *Shakespeare Bulletin.* He is also coauthor (with Schlueter) of *Reading Shakespeare in Performance: "King Lear"* and coeditor of *The Complete Works of St. Thomas More.*

FRANK OCCHIOGROSSO is Professor of English at Drew University. He is the editor of Alexander Nowell's *Catechism,* and his articles and reviews have appeared in *Shakespeare Quarterly, Literature/Film Quarterly, Shakespeare Bulletin, The Dictionary of Literary Biography,* and *The New Republic.* He has also worked as dramaturg for the New Jersey Shakespeare Festival.

MARVIN ROSENBERG, Professor Emeritus of Dramatic Art at the University of California, Berkeley, is the author of five books on Shakespeare: *The Masks of Othello, The Masks of King Lear, The Masks of Macbeth, The Masks of Hamlet,* and *The Adventures of a Shakespeare Scholar.* He has also had a festschrift, *Shakespearean Illuminations,* published in his honor by the University of Delaware Press.

JUNE SCHLUETER, Charles A. Dana Professor of English and Provost at Lafayette College, has written or edited books on Shakespeare, Arthur Miller, Peter Handke, and other aspects of dramatic literature. She is coeditor with James Lusardi of *Shakespeare Bulletin.*

Index

Adams, J. C., 7
AIDS plays, 40
Alexander, Bill, 40, 47–49, 51, 55
Allen, Patrick, 105
All or Nothing (Steinberg), 49
American Repertory Theater, 41
Anderson, Mary, 63–64, 69n. 15
anti-Semitism, 28, 30, 31, 34, 36, 37, 46, 49, 56
Arendt, Hannah: *The Origins of Totalitarianism*, 34
Aristotle: on money, 29
Arnold, Matthew: *Culture and Anarchy*, 30
As You Like It, 84, 86, 97. *See also under* Shakespeare, characters of
Atkins, Eileen, 88
Auden, W. H.: *The Dyer's Hand*, 38
aurality, 115–17

Barry, Spranger, 62
Bartholomeusz, Dennis, 18
Barton, John, 8, 19, 65
Bassano, Emilia, 51
Bate, Jonathan and Russell Jackson: *Shakespeare, An Illustrated Stage History*, 7
Beattie, Maureen, 116
Beckerman, Bernard, 7, 17
Bennett, Jill, 99
Bennett, Rodney, 105
Bergman, Ingmar, 20
Borman, Martin, 134
Bernhardt, Sarah, 62, 127
Berry, Ralph, 65, 134
Biggs, Murray, 40
Billington, Michael, 50
Bogdanov, Michael, 49, 64
Boose, Lynda E., 95
Bouchard, Thomas, 88
Boys in the Band, The (Crowley), 39
Bradbrook, Muriel, 18
Bradby, David, 18
Bradley, A. C., 18, 127

Branagh, Kenneth, 111
Brook, Peter, 20
Brown, John Russell, 8, 30
Brecht, Bertolt, 85
Brooke, Arthur: *Romeus and Juliet*, 108
Brown, John Russell, 131
Bulman, James, 11; (ed.) *Shakespeare, Theory, and Performance*, 8, 136
Burbach, Holly, 84
Burbage, Richard, 59, 119, 120
Burge, Stuart (director): *Julius Caesar*, 10, 93–103
Burt, Richard, 95

Calder, David, 50
Campbell, Mrs. Patrick, 63
Chamberlain, Richard, 99
Charney, Maurice, 93, 94; *Shakespeare's Roman Plays*, 95–96, 98–101
Chaste Maid in Cheapside, A (Middleton), 116
Chaucer, Geoffrey, 28
Church, Tony, 39
Cibber, Colley, 60
cinematography, 94
Cleese, John, 67
clothing, 48–49, 64
Cohen, Robert, 19
Constant Couple, The, 62
Corpus Christi plays, 28
Coursen, Herbert, 129
Crowl, Samuel, 95
Crowley, Martin: *The Boys in the Band*, 39
cross-dressing, 89–90
Culture and Anarchy (Arnold), 30
Cushman, Charlotte, 9, 69n. 8; in *Romeo and Juliet*, 61–63, 65, 68n. 5
Cushman, Susan, 62, 63

Damon and Pythias, 116
Danes, Claire, 109
David, Richard, 20
Davies, Marion, 89–90

143

144 INDEX

Death of Usury, or, The Disgrace of Usurers, 29
Dekker, Thomas: *The Honest Whore,* 117
De Marinis, Marco, 27
Dench, Judi, 39, 42, 43, 66, 81, 82, 104
Dessen, Allen, 7, 18, 76–78, 129
Dickens, Charles: *Oliver Twist,* 30; *Our Mutual Friend,* 30
Discourse upon Usury, A, 29
disguise, 84–92
Disraeli, Benjamin, 30
Donaldson, Peter S., 93
Doran, Gregory, 51, 55
Dyer's Hand, The (Auden), 38

Edgeworth, Maria, 30
Egoist, The, 87
Eliot, George, 30
Ellis-Fermor, Una, 18
England Shakespeare Company, 49
English Shakespeares (Holland), 49
Entertaining Mister Sloane (Orton), 39
Every Man In His Humor (Jonson), 120

Fascism, 49
Fielder, David, 115–16
Fielding, Emma, 85
Fishburne, Laurence, 111
Foakes, R. A., 76, 77
Forbes-Robertson, Johnston, 63, 131
formalism, 123–26
Frend, Andrew, 117

Garrick, David, 9, 73, 127; revises *Romeo and Juliet,* 60–62, 65
Geidt, Jeremy, 41
gender, 87, 87
ghetto: origins of, 52
Gielgud, John, 95, 134–35
Globe Theater (new), 18, 113–21
Gold, Jack, 82
Goldman, Michael, 19, 136
Gould, Michael, 115
Granville-Barker, Harley, 7, 17, 131
Greer, Germaine, 41
Gross, John, 56
Gurr, Andrew, 7, 18
Guthrie, Tyrone, 134

Halio, Jay, 130
Hamlet, 58, 59, 105–6, 111, 127, 129–30. *See also under* Shakespeare, characters of
Harbage, Alfred, 10, 123, 126
Harron, Mary, 41
Hattaway, Michael, 18
Hazlitt, William, 30, 128
Henry V, 115, 116
Henry VI, 65
Henry VIII, 113, 124
Heston, Charlton, 95, 101, 102
Higgins, Ken, 95, 99
Hodges, C. W., 7, 18
Hoffman, Dustin, 85, 86, 88
Holden, Stephen, 87, 88
Holland, Peter, 20, 54; *English Shakespeares,* 49
Holocaust, the, 47, 55
homosexuality, 38–41
Honest Whore, The (Dekker), 117
Hosley, Richard, 7
Howard, James, 60
Hoyle, Martin, 41
Hussey, Olivia, 66, 108, 109
Hytner, Nicholas, 105

Irving, Henry, 32–33, 63, 69n. 12

Jacobi, Derek, 105
Jaeger, Tom, 86
Jews, 28; assimilation of, 30; portrayal of, 27–31, 34; in Venice, 32. *See also under* Shakespeare, characters of
Johnson, Richard, 95
Jones, Ernest, 132
Jongh, Nicholas de, 39
Jonson, Ben, 51, 229; *Every Man In His Humor,* 120
Jorgens, Jack, 95
Joseph, Bertram L., 10, 19, 123–24, 126
Julius Caesar, 118; Burge production of, 10; Mankiewicz production of, 106. *See also under* Shakespeare, characters of

Kean, Edmund, 30, 62, 128
Keats, John, 84, 86, 91, 92
Kemble, Charles, 62
Kemble, John Philip, 61, 73
Kemp, William, 120
Kennedy, Dennis: *Looking at Shakespeare,* 20

Index

King, Thomas, 18
King Lear, 58, 59, 62, 111, 127
Knight, Wilson, 132

Laing, F. D., 85
Lamb, Charles, 127
Lane, Anthony, 87
Lange, Jessica, 86
Lapotaire, Jane, 81, 82, 109
Leach, Joseph, 62
Lefton, Sue, 117
Lepage, Robert, 20
Levenson, Jill, 62
Lloyd, Harold, 88
Looking at Shakespeare (Kennedy), 20
Luhrmann, Baz, 108
Lusardi, James and June Schlueter, eds.: *Shakespeare Bulletin*, 9
Luscombe, Tim, 49
lyric poetry, 59

Macaulay, Alistair, 50, 55
Macbeth, 9, 59, 71–82, 104, 109–10. *See also under* Shakespeare, characters of
Macklin, Charles, 30
Macready, William Charles, 62
Mankiewicz, Joseph, 106, 110
Marlowe, Christopher, 60
McDiarmid, Ian, 52–53
McGuire, Philip: *Speechless Dialect*, 67
McKellen, Ian, 80, 82, 109, 110
Measure for Measure, 97, 133, 134
Merchant of Venice, 8, 9, 27–44, 47–56, 59, 67, 107–8, 111, 117. *See also under* Shakespeare, characters of
Middleton, Thomas: *A Chaste Maid in Cheapside*, 116
Midsummer Night's Dream, A, 59, 62
Miller, Jonathan, 33–35, 47, 50, 67, 108
Mirren, Helen, 82
Modjeska, Helen, 63
Much Ado About Nothing, 111
Muir, Kenneth, 18
Mullan, John, 87
Mulryne, J. R. and Margaret Shewring: *Shakespeare's Globe Rebuilt*, 7

Nathan, David, 47
Need for Words, The (Rodenburg), 135
Nelson, Jeanette, 115
Nielsen, Asta, 89

Nightingale, Benedict, 51
Nunn, Trevor, 82, 104, 109; directs *Twelfth Night*, 10, 84–92

Odell, George C. D., 63; *Shakespeare From Betterton to Irving*, 7
Oliver Twist (Dickens), 30
Olivier, Lawrence, 132; as Macbeth, 71; production of *The Merchant of Venice*, 33, 34, 50, 108
Origins of Totalitarianism, The (Arendt), 34
Orrell, John, 7
Orton, Joe: *Entertaining Mister Sloane*, 39
Othello, 111, 127, 132
Otway, Thomas: *The Rise and Fall of Caius Marius*, 60
Our Mutual Friend (Dickens), 30

Parker, Oliver, 111
performance criticism, 27, 123–36
Platter, Sir Thomas, 113
Players of Shakespeare, 8, 19
Plowright, Joan, 90
Polanski, Roman, 82, 109
Porter, Eric, 109, 110
Pritchard, Hannah, 73

Rich, Frank, 40
Richard II, 59. *See also under* Shakespeare, characters of
Richard III, 104, 125
Rigg, Diana, 99
Ripley, John, 18
Rise and Fall of Caius Marius, The (Otway), 60
Ritter, Sonia, 117
Robards, Jason, 95
Rodenburg, Patsy: *The Need for Words*, 135
Romeo and Juliet, 58–68, 85, 108. *See also under* Shakespeare, characters of
Romeus and Juliet (Brooke), 108
Rosenberg, Marvin, 7–11, 17, 73
Rothschild family, 30, 34, 36
Rowe, Stephen, 41
Royal Shakespeare Company (RSC), 39, 40, 50, 52, 59, 64, 65, 82, 85, 104, 109, 111, 134
Russell, William, 116

Rutter, Carol, 8
Rylance, Mark, 116

Sanders, Wilbur, 29
script omission, 104–12
Scurfield, Matthew, 116
Sellars, Peter, 36, 67
setting, 65–68
Shakespeare, William:
—characters of: *As You Like It:* Jaques, 97. *Hamlet:* Hamlet, 31, 62. *Henry V:* Falstaff, 62. *Julius Caesar:* Brutus, 97, 106, 107; Casca, 96; Cassius, 96, 97; Cinna, 97; Marc Antony, 101, 102, 106. *Merchant of Venice:* Antonio, 29, 35, 37–44; Bassanio, 37, 38, 40–43; Duke, 35; Gratiano, 29, 39; Jessica, 35, 49, 50, 54; Launcelot Gobbo, 50; Lorenzo, 35, 49, 54; Portia, 37–43, 46 n. 25; Salerio, 37, 38, 41, 42; Shylock, 27–36, 43, 44, 50, 52–55, 62, 107–8; Solanio, 37, 51, 52, 54; Tubal, 53–54. *Macbeth:* Lady Macbeth, 73–82, 89; Macbeth, 71–82, 89. *Richard II:* Richard II, 62. *Romeo and Juliet:* Friar Lawrence, 61, 65; Juliet, 60–68, 111; Lady Montague, 60; Romeo, 60–68; Rosaline, 60, 62, 65; Viola, 62. *The Taming of the Shrew:* Petruchio, 67. *Titus Andronicus:* Aaron the Moor, 31. *Twelfth Night:* Andrew, 91–92; Antonio, 87; Cesario, 85–89, 91, 92; Feste, 88; Ganymede, 85; Hermione, 91; Jessica, 86; Leontes, 91; Malvolio, 86, 87, 90, 91, 105, 110; Olivia, 86, 87, 90–92, 110; Orlando, 84–86; Orsino, 85–89, 91; Rosalind, 85; Sebastian, 86–88, 90; Viola, 84, 85, 87–90, 97.
—performances of, 27–44
—and use of words, 15–26
Shakespeare and the Actors (Sprague), 129
Shakespeare and the Authority of Performance (Worthen), 8, 67, 136
Shakespeare From Betterton to Irving (Odell), 7
Shakespeare Bulletin (ed. Lusardi and Schlueter), 9, 67
Shakespeare & Company, 86
Shakespeare on the English Stage, 1900–1964 (Trewin), 7
Shakespeare, An Illustrated Stage History (Bate and Jackson), 7
Shakespeare in Love, 84, 85, 88
Shakespeare Revolution, The (Styan), 136
Shakespeare and the Sense of Performance (Thompson and Thompson), 135–36
Shakespeare on the Stage (Speaight), 7
Shakespeare Survey, 40
Shakespeare, Theory, and Performance (ed. Bulman), 8, 136
Shakespeare's Globe Rebuilt (Mulryne and Shewring), 7
Shakespeare's Roman Plays: The Function of Imagery in the Drama (Charney), 95–96, 98–99, 100, 101
Shaw, Fiona, 62
Sher, Anthony, 47
Siddons, Sarah, 73, 127
Smith, Clarence, 117
Smith, Irwin, 7
Sorban, Andrea, 41, 43, 44
Speaight, Robert: *Shakespeare on the Stage,* 7
Speechless Dialect (McGuire), 67
Sprague, Arthur Colby, 7, 11, 17; *Shakespeare and the Actors,* 129
staging, 64–68
Stein, Peter, 20
Steinberg, Jonathan: *All or Nothing,* 49
Steinem, Gloria, 86
Stewart, Patrick, 47, 54
Stoppard, Tom, 58
Strehler, Giorgio, 20
Stride, John, 66
Stubbs, Imogen, 88, 90
Sturgess, Keith, 18
Styan, John: *The Shakespeare Revolution,* 136
subjectivity, 31
Suzman, Janet, 109, 110

Tabori, Georg, 36
Taming of the Shrew, The, 67. See also under Shakespeare, characters of
Taylor, Paul, 41, 51
Terry, Ellen, 63
Thacker, David, 50, 111
Thaw, John, 110
Theaters Act (1968), 39
Third Reich, 35, 45n. 18

Thompson, Marvin and Ruth: *Shakespeare and the Sense of Performance,* 136
Thomson, Peter, 18
Titus Andronicus, 31. *See also under* Shakespeare, characters of
Tootsie, 85, 86
Tree, Ellen, 62
Trewin, J. C.: *Shakespeare on the English Stage, 1900–1964,* 7
Trollope, Anthony, 30
Twelfth Night, 105; Nunn production of, 10, 84–92. *See also under* Shakespeare, characters of
Two Gentlemen of Verona, 48, 116
Tynan, Kenneth, 50, 82

usury, 29

Vaughn, Robert, 95
Venora, Diane, 62

Victorians/Victorian age, 30–33
Vitagraph studios, 88

Wells, Stanley, 20
Westwell, Raymond, 54
Whitney, Leonard, 66
Williams, Gary Jay, 18
Williamson, Nicol, 82, 109
Winter, William, 63
Winter's Tale, 91, 115, 119–20
Wise, Herbert, 106
Wood, Clive, 85
Worthen, William, 9, 11, 19, 66–67; *Shakespeare and the Authority of Performance,* 8, 67, 136
Wright, William, 88

Zefferelli, Franco, 66, 108